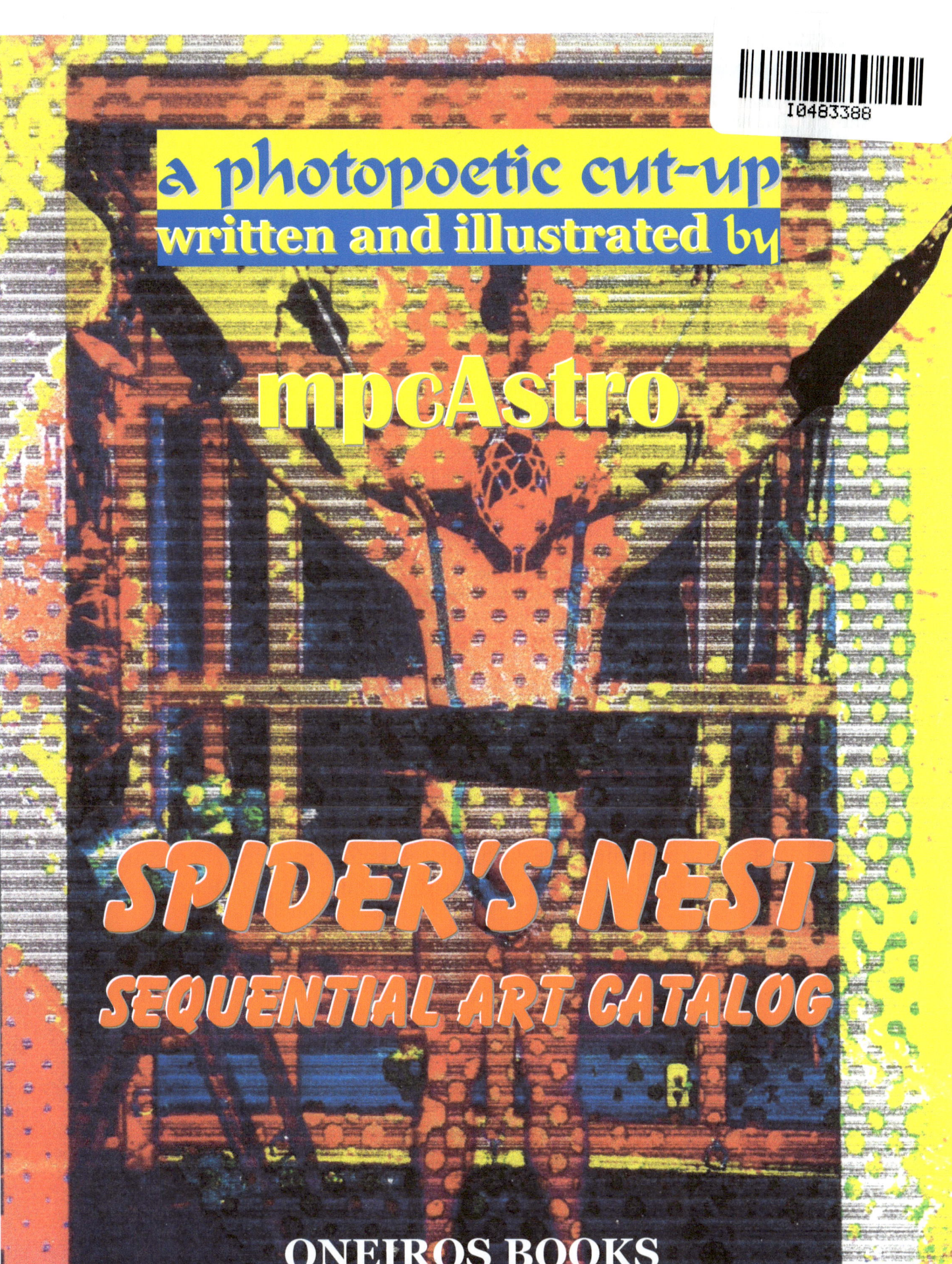

a photopoetic cut-up
written and illustrated by

mpcAstro

SPIDER'S NEST
SEQUENTIAL ART CATALOG

ONEIROS BOOKS

From 1980 thru March, 2014, cut-ups from *Spider's Nest* first appeared in Diane Gage's *Antenna Poetry & Graphics* and Community Arts Gallery, *both* San Diego, CA; Ann Erickson's *Tight Magazine,* Guerneville, CA; Fred Engels' *Shattered Wig Review,* Baltimore, MD; Lakeland Center for Creative Art's *Onionhead Literary Quarterly,* Lakeland, FL; Christian Nelson's *Kumquat Meringue,* Rockford, IL; Tim Scott's *Dream International Quarterly,* Chicago, IL; Sharon Wysocki's *The Wire,* Dearborn Heights, MI; John M. Bennett's *Lost & Found Times,* Columbus, OH; Findhorn Foundation's *One Earth Quarterly,* Forres, Morayshire, Scotland; Pat Lei's sick *Head Magazine* handout and Daedalus Publishing Co.'s, *Between the Cracks: an Anthology of Kinky Verse,* edited by Gavin Dillard, *both* Los Angeles, CA; Beyond Baroque Literary Art Center's *1998 Visual Poetry Exhibition* (co-sponsored by Poets & Writers, Inc. and the Los Angeles County Museum of Art), Venice, CA; other L.A.-area galleries: *Van Go's Ear* (Venice) and Dr. Susan Block's *Speakeasy* (downtown); Tampa, FL-area, galleries: *Kicks on Seventh Avenue, Nude Nite, Tampa Artists Emporium, Old Hyde Park Art Center,* and Daphne Haines' *Capricorn Studios* (Ybor City); Ben John Smith's online *Horror Sleaze Trash,* as well his print comix art & poetry anthology, *FUCK YOU PAY ME,* Tullamarine, Victoria, Australia; TableGlock Press's *Boscombe Revolution,* Bournemouth, England; with chaptered flash-cycle vignettes bopped into an *operotica,* "Nidus Plexus: Immortal Fungus," included in another Oneiros Books (Neath, Wales), imprint, *CUT UP! Method Anthology*, co-edited by A. D. Hitchin and Joe Ambrose. This Art Catalog is based on the 48-paged saddle-stitch bound booklet, *Spider's Nest,* put out by eMCee/LMnO Press (1997), Venice, California; subtitled, *within the Shadow of Soma.* (U.S. Library of Congress control no.: 98161595)

mpcAstro is an artist who waxes oppoetic near the Gulf of Mexico's teal-tongued waters lapping at the peninsular underside of Florida's powdered sugar shores where he consummated his thirty-year *opus interruptus* of photopoetics, *SPIDER'S NEST Sequential Art Catalog,* privately published (OᵒPRESS, 2011) in a Limited Edition of 100 before re-printed here, thanks to Dave ("D. M.") Mitchell, Founding Publisher, Oneiros Books.

This amplifiction's tri-agonists — Illustra Kix, Amrita Amanita, and Dr. Mortsac — are loosely modeled on the author's resonated 666-day passion role-play with the erstwhile Los Angeles-based dominatrices Ilsa Strix and Izabella Sol, before 2001, after which time the trinity dissolved like powdered sugar into The Gulf along with their pre[de]vious millennial identities.

www.paraphiliamagazine.com/oneirosbooks

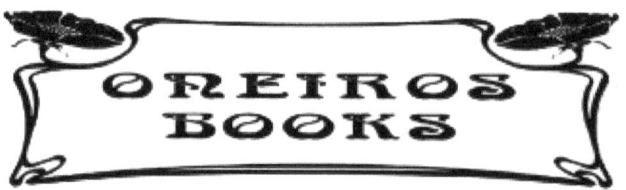

AD ASTRA PER ASPERA
(to the stars thru difficulties)

S.P.I.D.E.R.'S

N.E.S.T

At the Temple of the Virgin at Ephesus

SPIDER'S NEST
SEQUENTIAL ART CATALOG

a photopoetic cut-up
written and illustrated by

mpcAstro

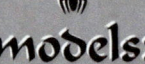

models:
- **Ilsa Strix**
- **Izabella Sol**   slave m

- bondagettes:

courtesy of *Chez Ricochet:*
House of Appropriation

an
ONEIROS BOOKS
operotica

First Edition   March 8, 2014

Contents

~ for Erin, who made our nest an aerie ~ Mike

Prelude
VERSO/RECTO
Diptych

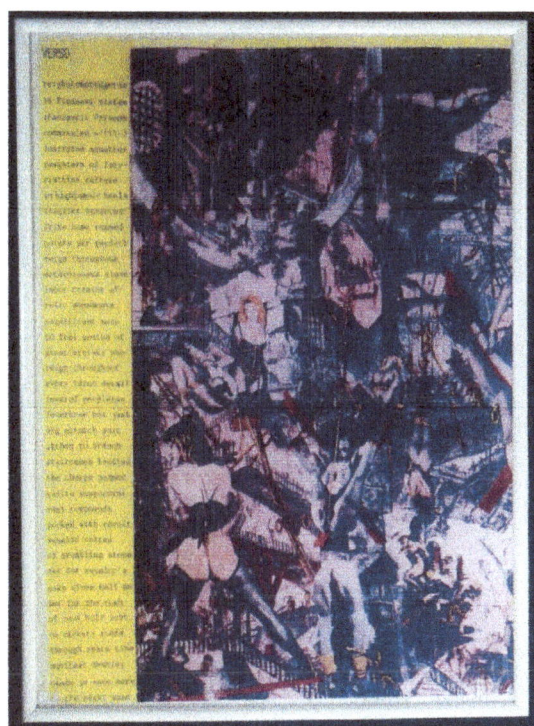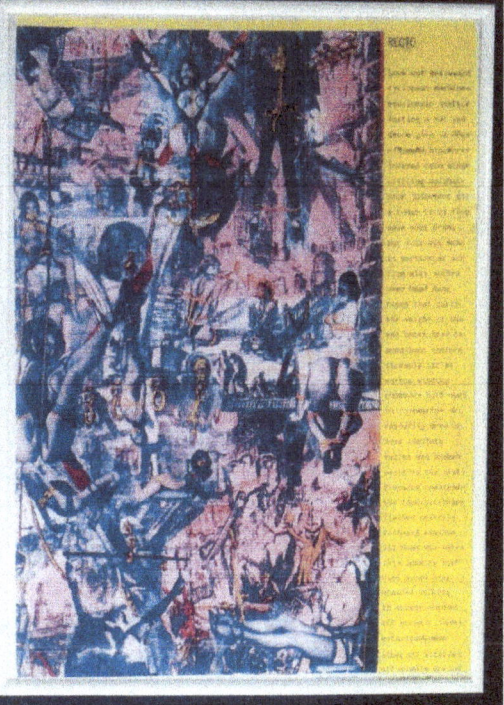

The conveyance station for Automated Linguistics jumped track. Its monstrous cam ajam. As they assessed damage control from the cupola's lofty vantage, her indentured epistemologist, Dr. Mortsac, was nudged by his trans**genre**d *Venus Ex Machina*, the Webstress Illustra von Kix, in all her pan**text**ual plumery: "Less epi**pseud**ic, more epi**sod**ic, my dear doc**tor**, lest we embrace Chaos." *Does she suspect my Phantom Limbs—Heresy and Anarchy?*

Picking up the gauntlet, the erstwhile **Erosopher** inwardly vowed to, thereinafter, amplify the logic of his metrics through the **pixeLucinatious** subconch.sys of the **Nidus Plexus** where creature may frequent Creatrix via **hiero**conversation...a circular, organic hypertext where artifact commingles with Architect in a dervish dance of opposites spooning into a dialectical ball of fire: the fabled **Omen Globe**—the elusive *Disposable* **Singularity.**

Episodic enough, Ms. Kix? "Kink is our business, Mistress. This is only a **kink**," said he with a toothy grin. *I see you*, did she, *Venus Fitzgerald Crisis!*

re:photomontagerie
16 Piranesi plates
:*Fantastic Prisons*
commingled w/(il-)
*lust*rated squatter
daughters of *laby-*
*rinth*ine culture
in highiambic heels
disquiet dungeons
drive home pumped
points per perfect
reign throughout
archcolossus slave
labor creator of
relic monuments
magnificent made
to feel genius of
great artists who
reign throughout
every idiot detail
fevered perplexus
fevertree not just
big scratch post
itches to branch
staircases leading
the charge beamed
vaults supporting
vast compounds
pocked with revolt
squalid suites
of crumbling stone
not for squalor's
sake alone hell no
but for the rush
of root hold lost
on rickety roads
through space time
manifest destiny
heads us once more
to the right page

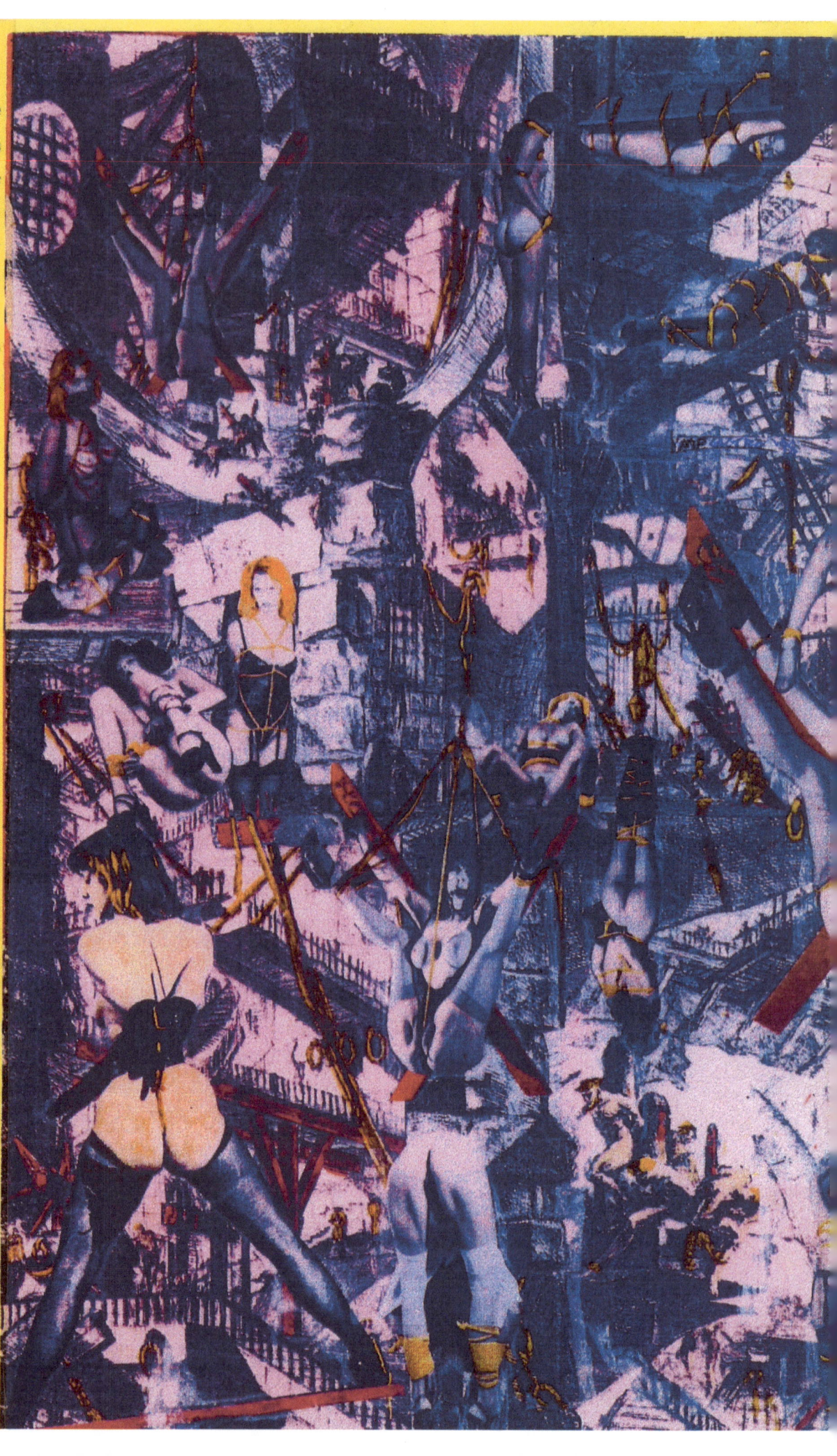

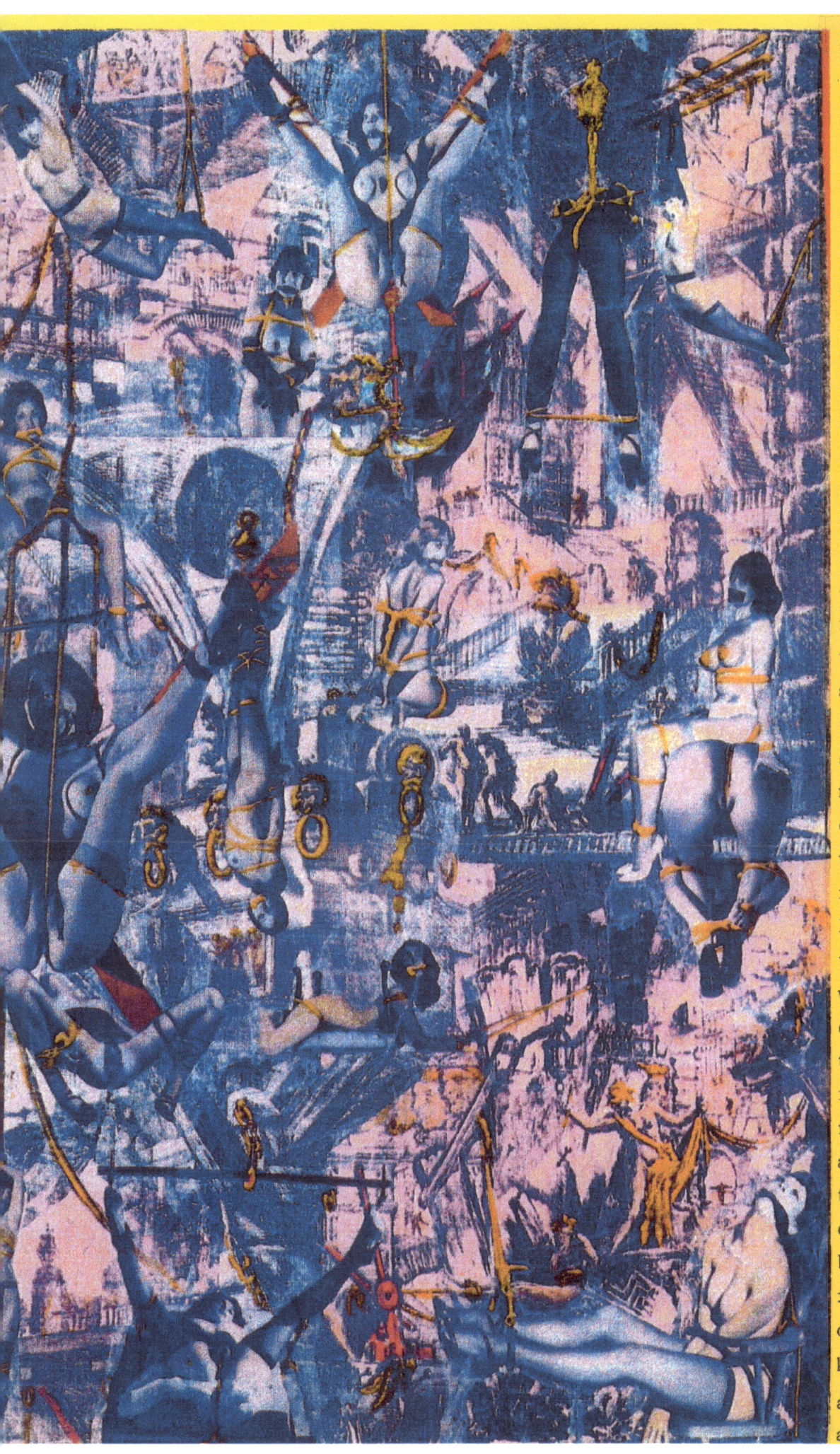

Look out belowward
cyclopean machines
neoclassic justice
busting a nut gad
deuce give us *Déus*
ofMamaMachinaWorks
lowered onto stage
piffling epiphany
poor judgement day
a tough titty flop
save your drama
for your big mama
in particular sag
from airy arches
over head hang
ropes that carry
the weight of the
sap heavy hive in
pendulous torture
sickenly lit by
narrow windows
chambers half open
to rosemarine sky
revealing more or
less complete
vaults and broken
walls in the misty
distance coextends
the feverpitchtree
flushed severely
redboard abandon
all hope who enter
this burning bush
dumb asses bray
branded balking
in steamy shadows
off stage a choral
katzenjamhammer
after all after sex
all animals are sad

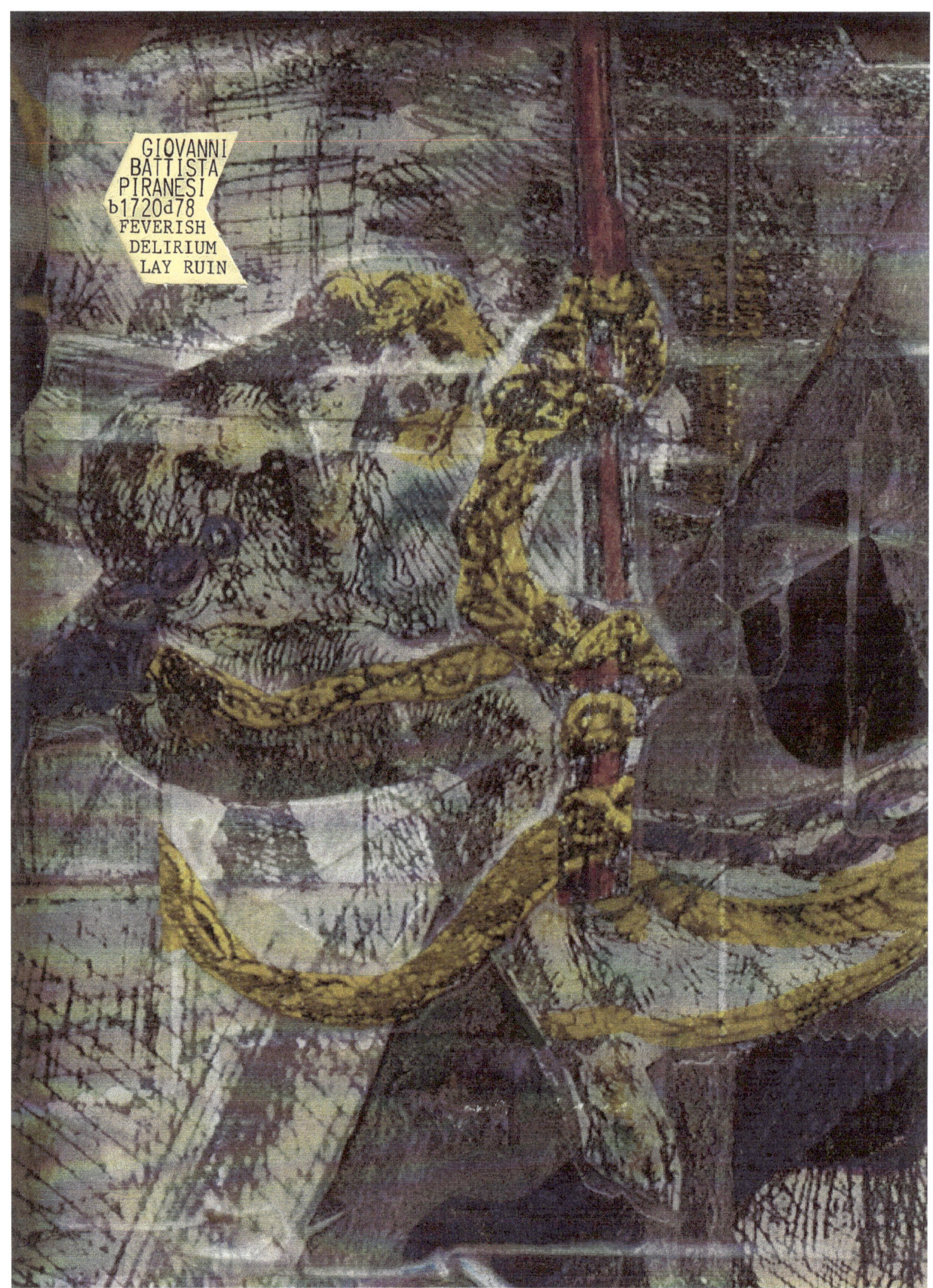

GIOVANNI
BATTISTA
PIRANESI
b1720d78
FEVERISH
DELIRIUM
LAY RUIN

Proto-prints

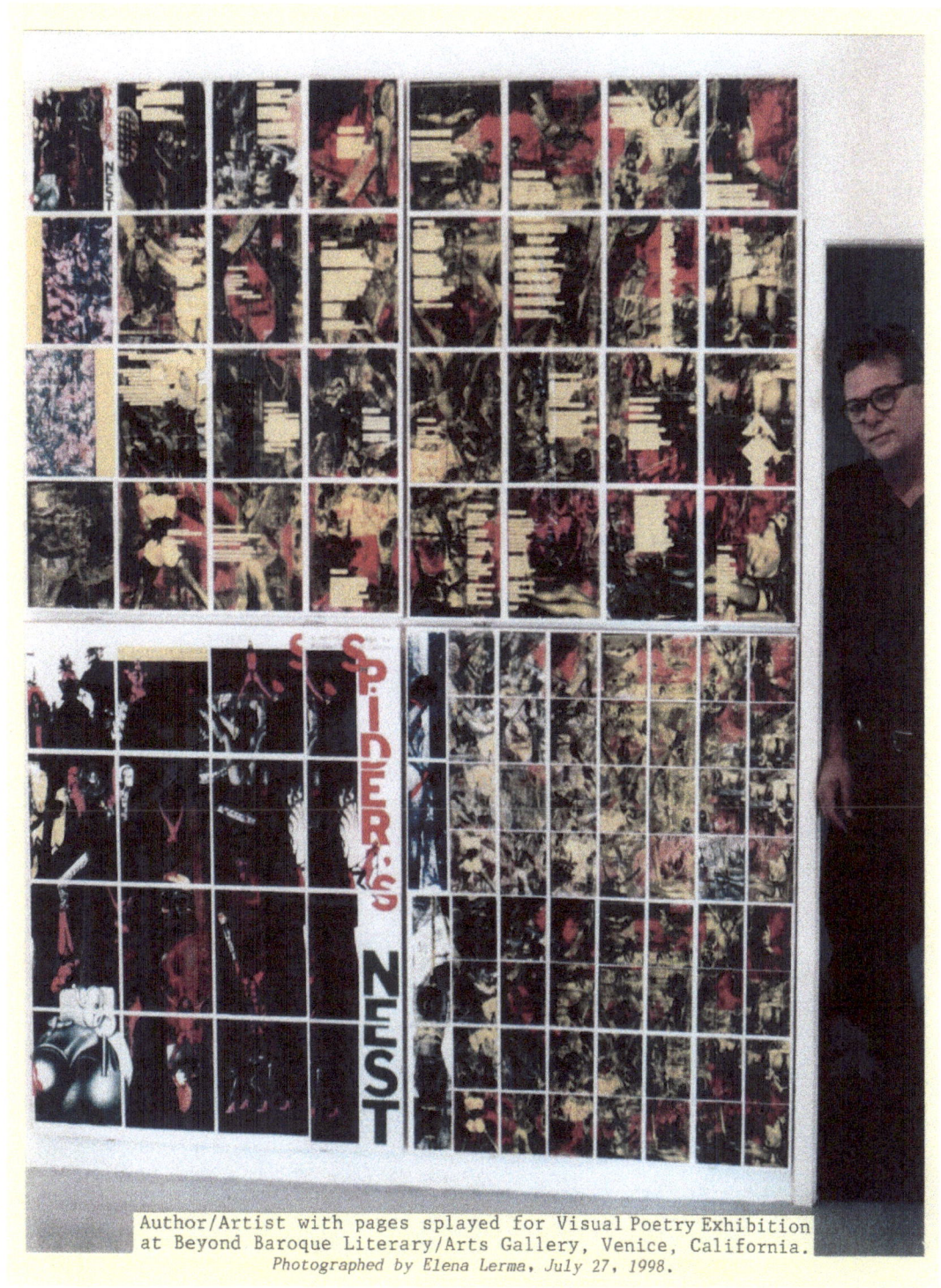

Author/Artist with pages splayed for Visual Poetry Exhibition
at Beyond Baroque Literary/Arts Gallery, Venice, California.
Photographed by Elena Lerma, July 27, 1998.

Doctoral machinations went viral. An infection of incantations was introduced into Nidus Plexus's vocabulary, retooling its quack dialectic to run a cascading tessellation of autonomous phantasmagoria. *Avant-Arabesque!*

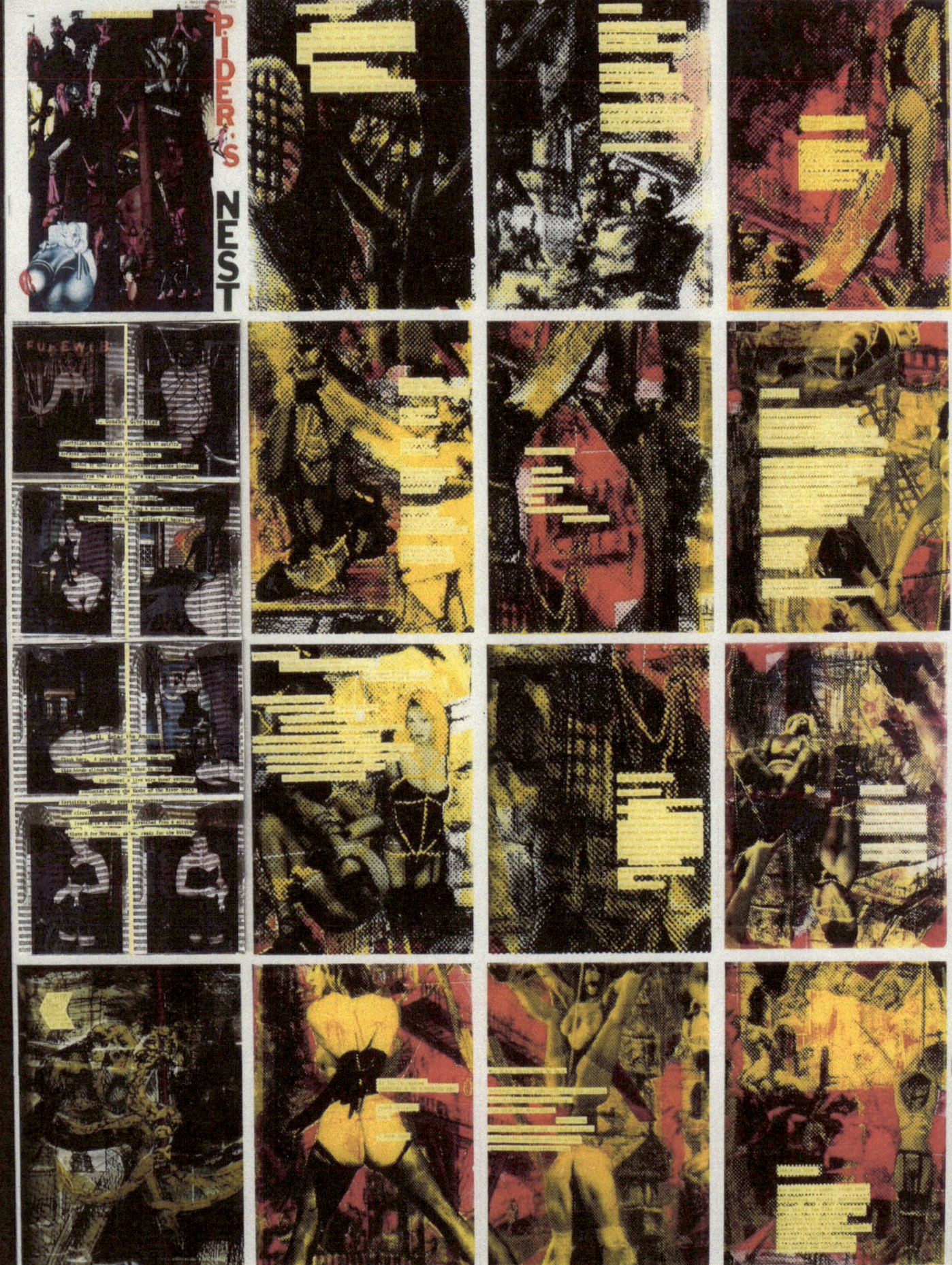

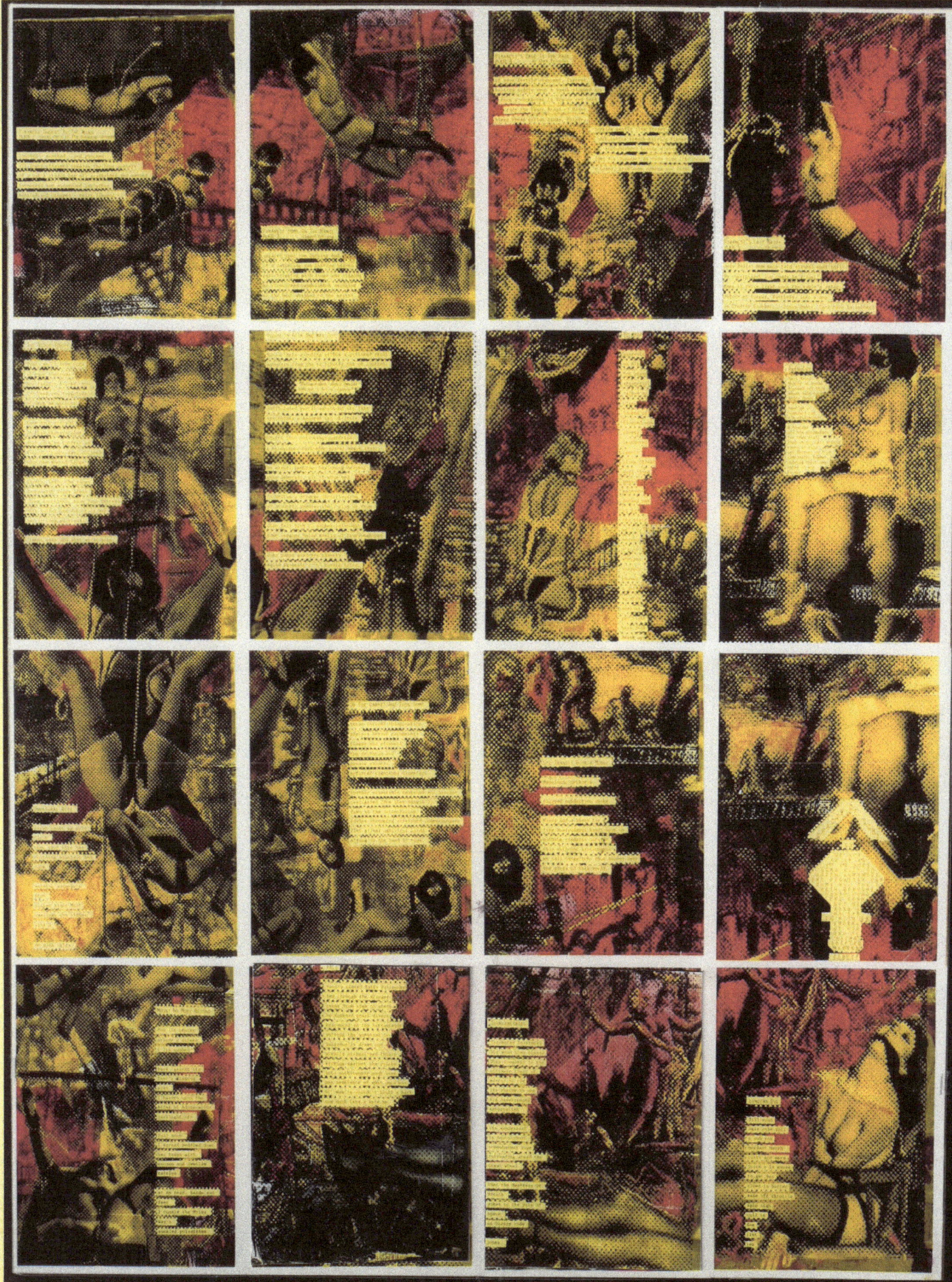

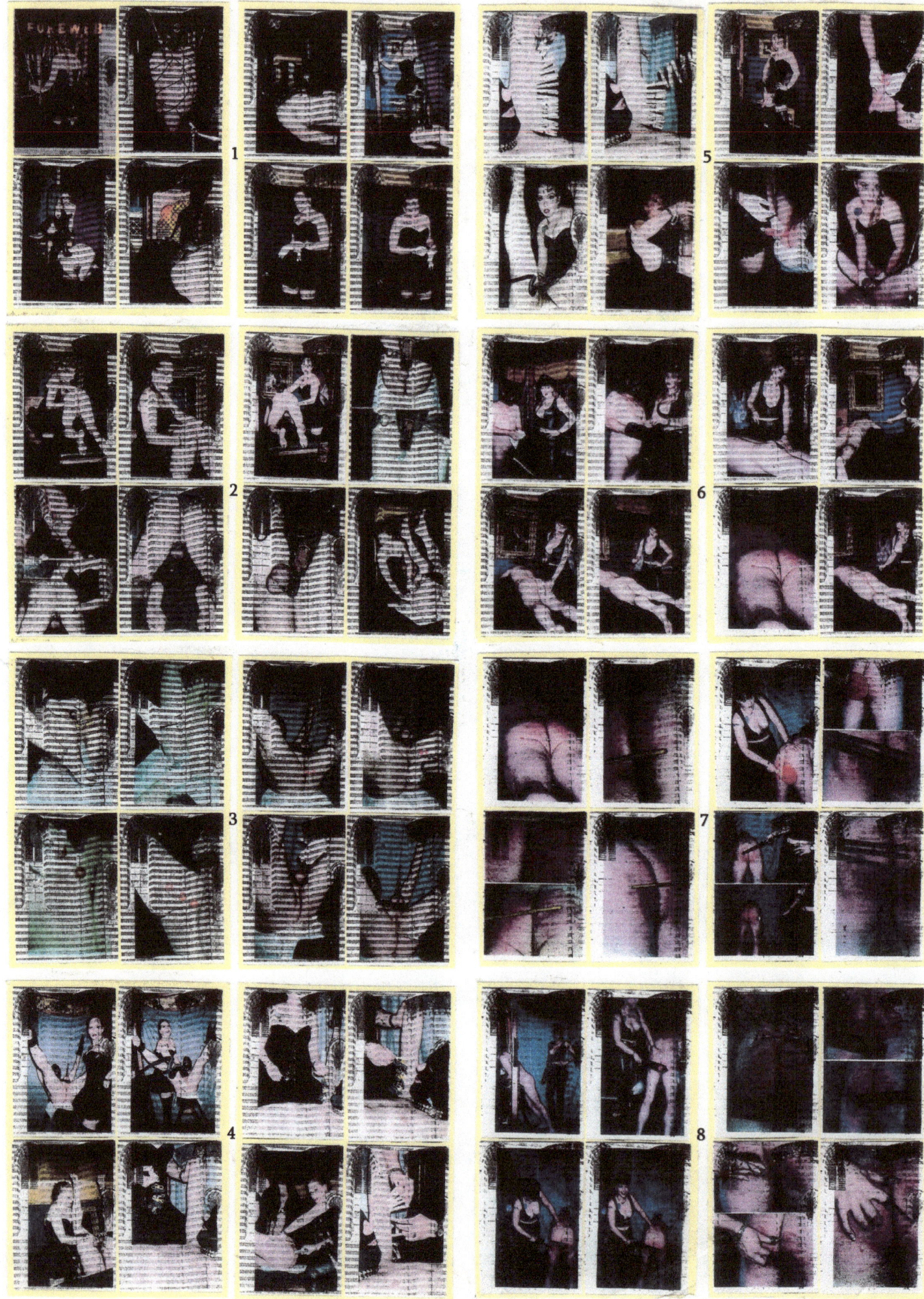

Foreweb
OLD WORLD NEW
featuring Illustra von Kix

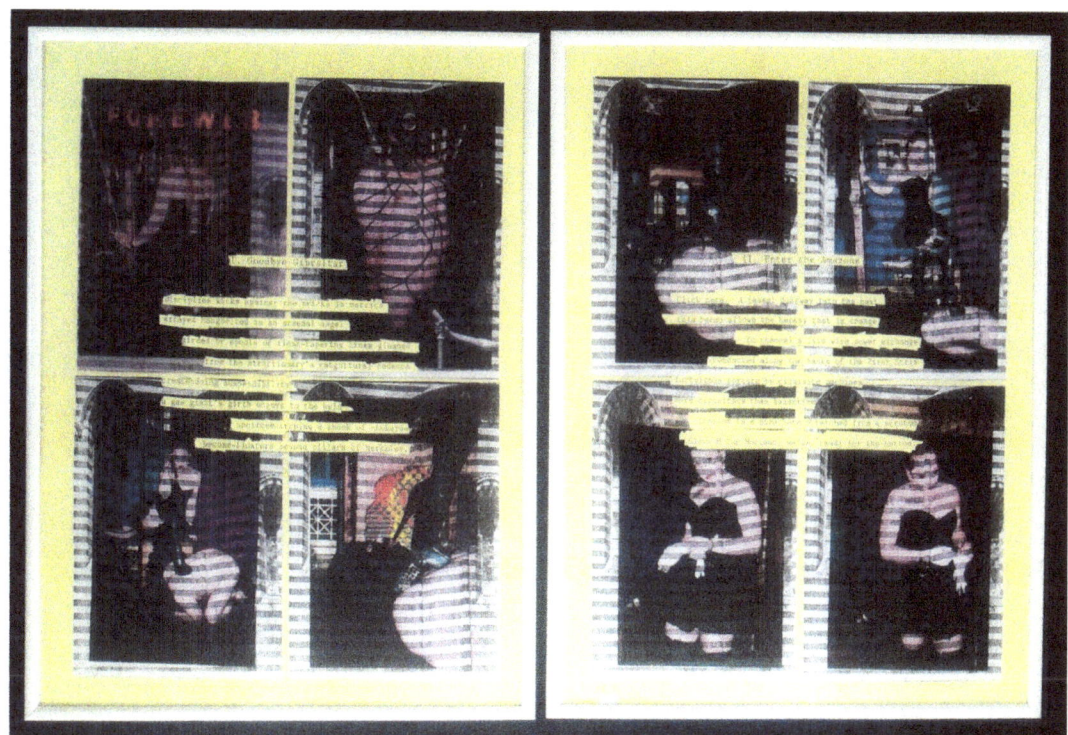

I first met the Webstress by appointment on a blistering First of July afternoon at her "happy"—Los Feliz—home's dungeon with a portfolio of my *photo cut-ups.* I explained, while she leafed through the illustrated poems, that it was my intention to "flesh in" the exoskeletal catalog she had in her hands with genuine gotherotic scenery. She agreed, in exchange for modeling scenes, to enweb the artist for 666 days while the camera could be tossed from slave to Illustrix to crew, all shooting scenes on the mat with Erato, Muse of Lyric, in a **no holds barred** grapple of metronomic servitude.

To submit one's **self**—Art's ultimate price.

Did I have the *cajones?* Sounded better than holing up in a flop with an Underwood "typer" from Goodwill and *broke dick*...I've done **that** for art: getting **it** broke off and on a fork fed me. The folio aside, Illustra handed me a clip boarded "Dialog Sheet" with pen. I scribbled "**no _holes_ barred.**"

13

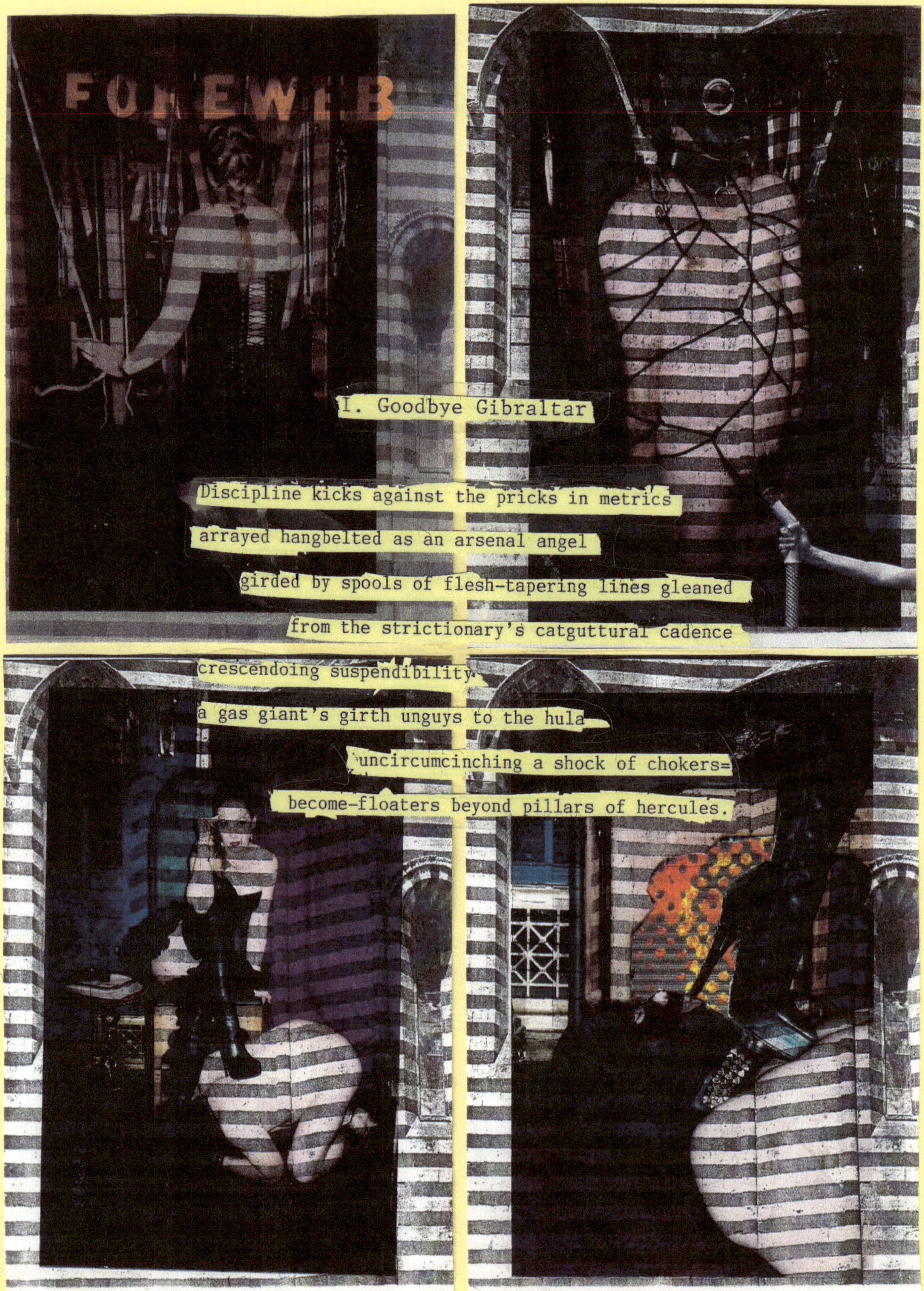

FOREWEB

I. Goodbye Gibraltar

Discipline kicks against the pricks in metrics

arrayed hangbelted as an arsenal angel

girded by spools of flesh-tapering lines gleaned

from the strictionary's catguttural cadence

crescendoing suspendibility·

a gas giant's girth unguys to the hula

uncircumcinching a shock of chokers=

become-floaters beyond pillars of hercules.

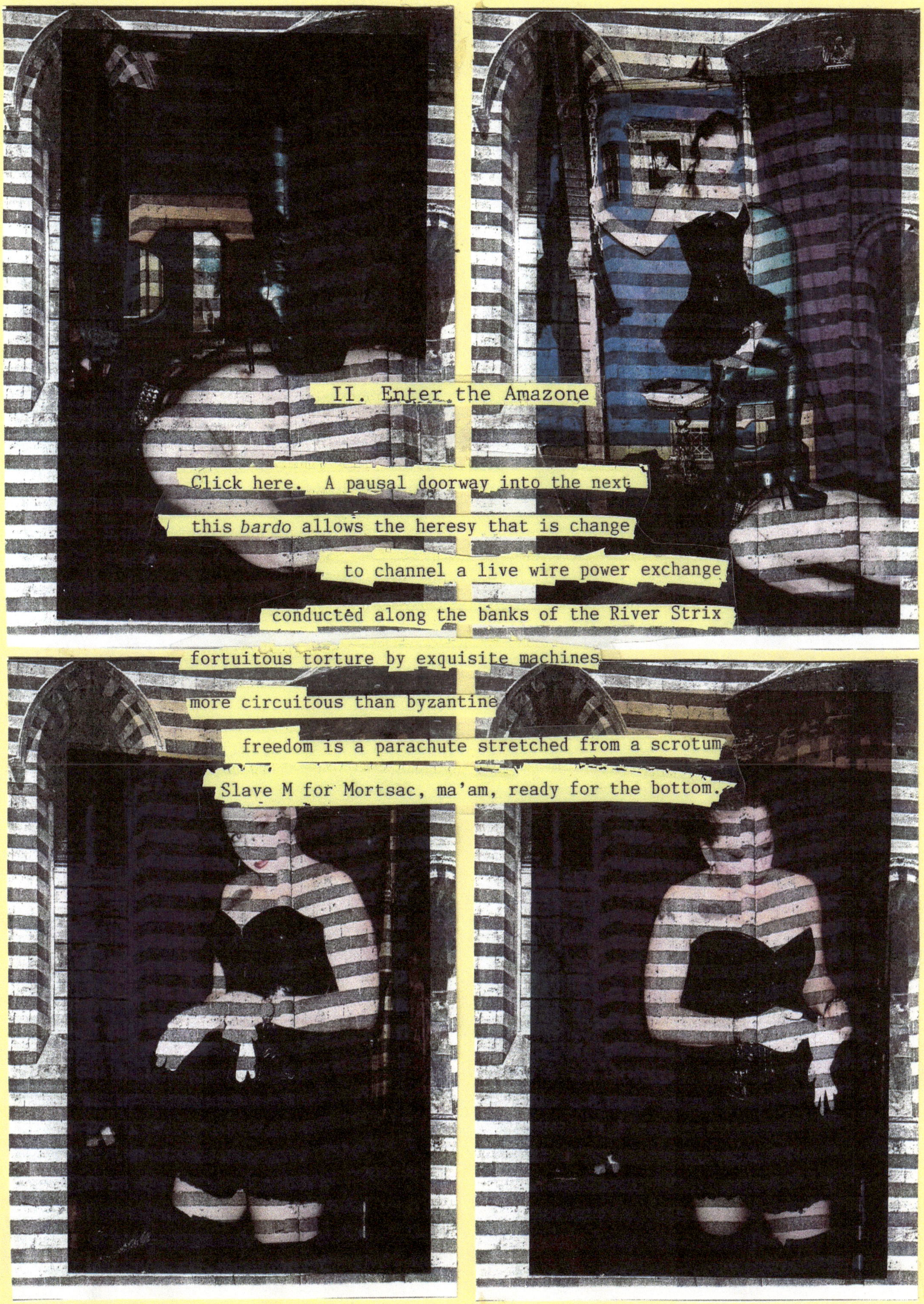

II. Enter the Amazone

Click here. A pausal doorway into the next
this *bardo* allows the heresy that is change
to channel a live wire power exchange
conducted along the banks of the River Strix
fortuitous torture by exquisite machines
more circuitous than byzantine
freedom is a parachute stretched from a scrotum
Slave M for Mortsac, ma'am, ready for the bottom.

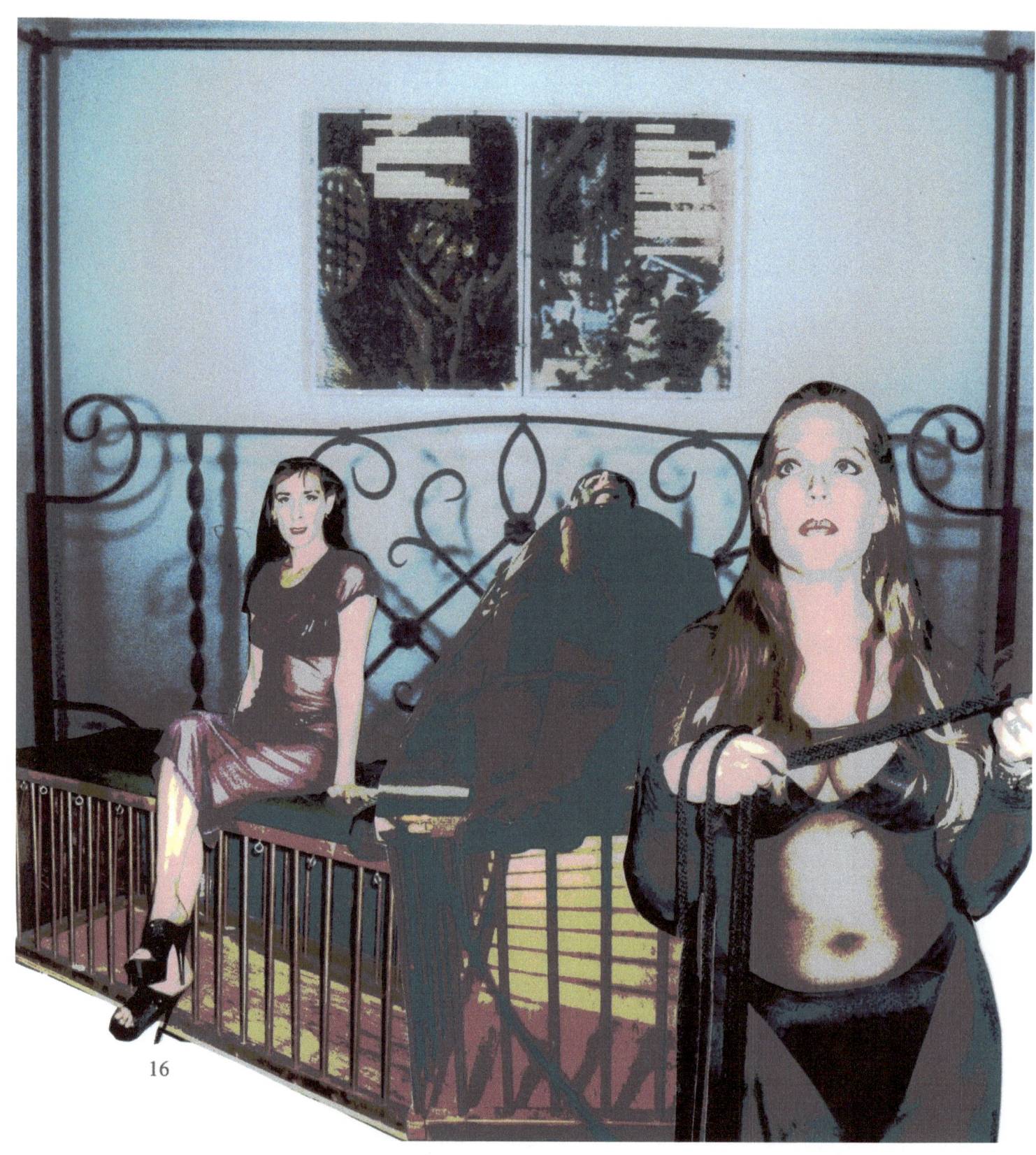

16

Chapter 1
COCK CROW
Diptych

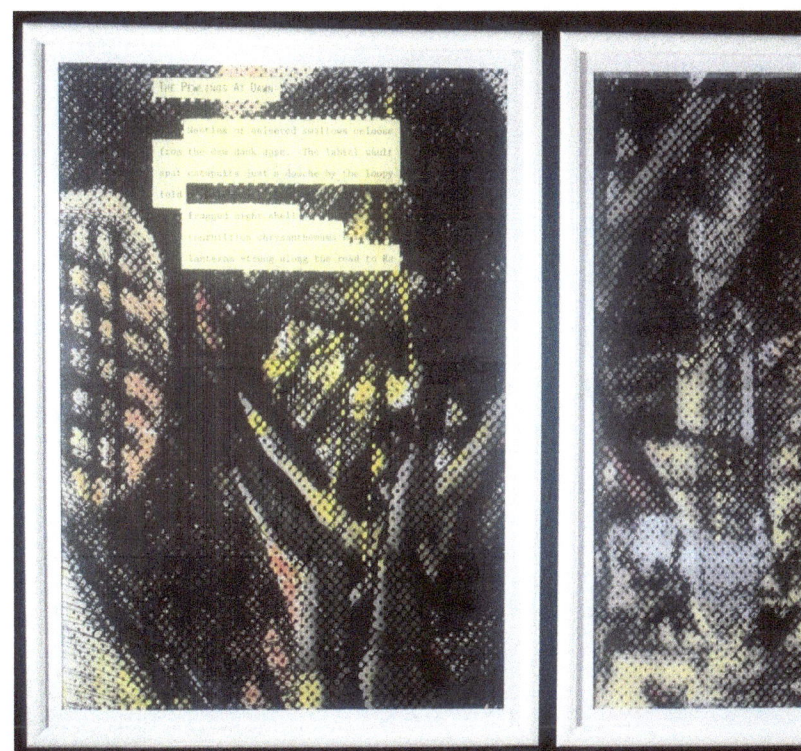

    The artist awoke from a florescent dream of fantastically frantic butterflies—orange, black, silver-yellow and peach blush—by the thousands scrambling to tear out from black pixelknit cocoons. One after another, each winged emergent, within seconds of first flight, would decorate a ubiquitous web that seemed to canopy the whole cocoonscape, so that sky and earth to horizon had become a kaleidoscopic vibration of vivacious panic.

    Eyes open to vitreous opacities transmogrified into a Boschian parade of buffoonery . . . hilarious **mass destruction** hysteria. *Mo'f'er! Rub these* **endoftheworld** *floaters out of your eyes, dude...Hello?* Arms seem to be sewn to sides. *Wha' duh?* Legs encased in...silk? Torso, immobilized as well. *Fug!*

    "Rise and shine, Cloudcuckoohead..." *Lustra?* "Hope you don't mind me holding vigil...oh, **and** my sis', *Am'*—**Amanita** to you. How do you find the body bag we slid you into as you *slept?* Comfy?" *Yeah, snug as a bug; wh'up, Bit'h?*

THE PEWLINGS AT DAWN

Nestles of quivered swallows unloose
from the dew dank apse. The labial vault
spat catapults just a douche by the loopy
fold

fragged night shell
tourbillion chrysanthemums
lanterns strung along the road to Ra

RIGGED VEHICLE

girded by young birch bark and
silver to the teeth
a car, blazing astral gardens

did scout up giddy alps
of hovering ziggurats railed
by spunkincensed trees abust

with nether roots forth frothing
up soma'shrooms quaffed by imps
the swollen ones piss ambrosia:

appointed toadskin anointments.

framed wrought iron bed

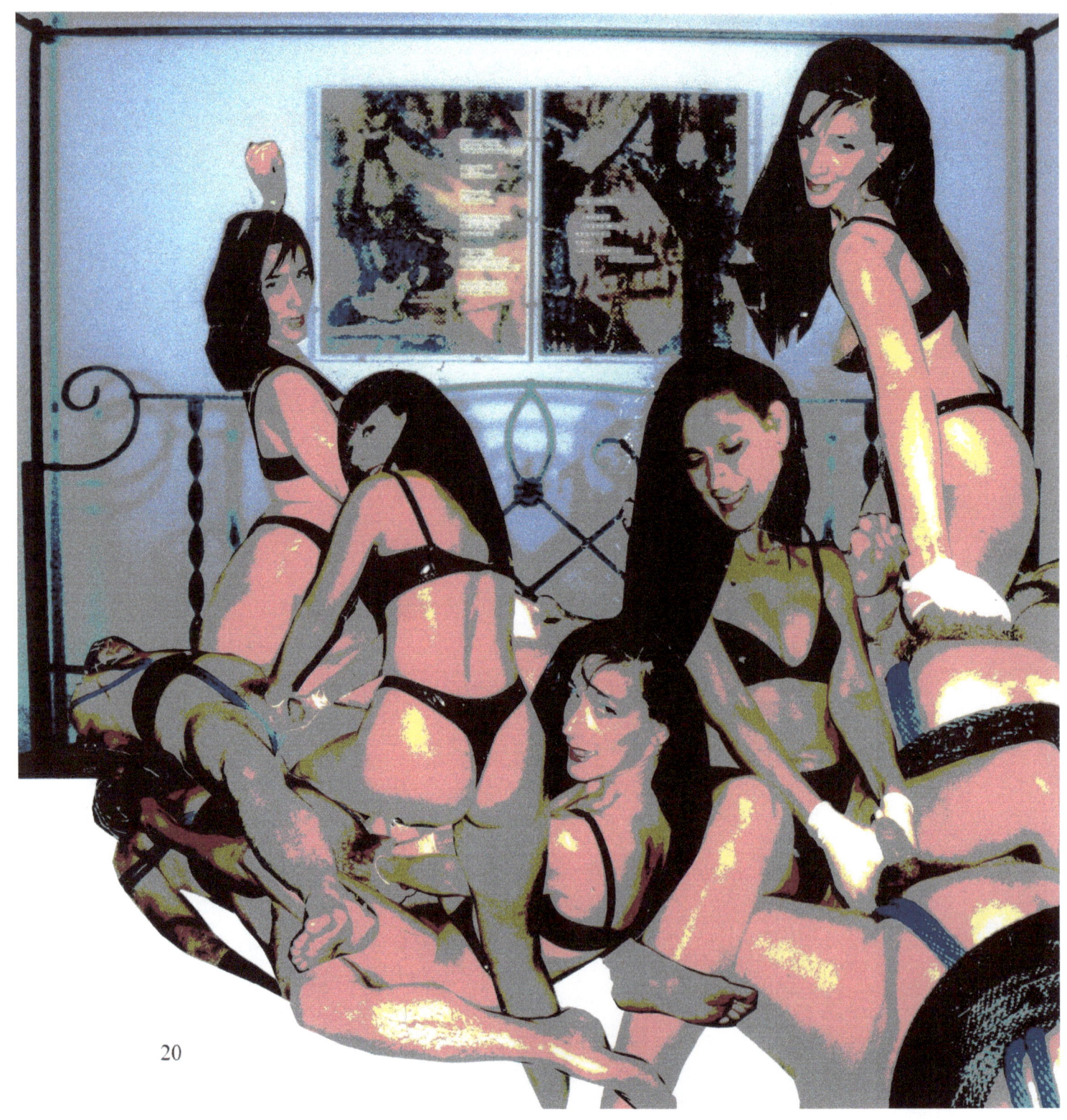

Chapter 2
WAYLAID
Diptych

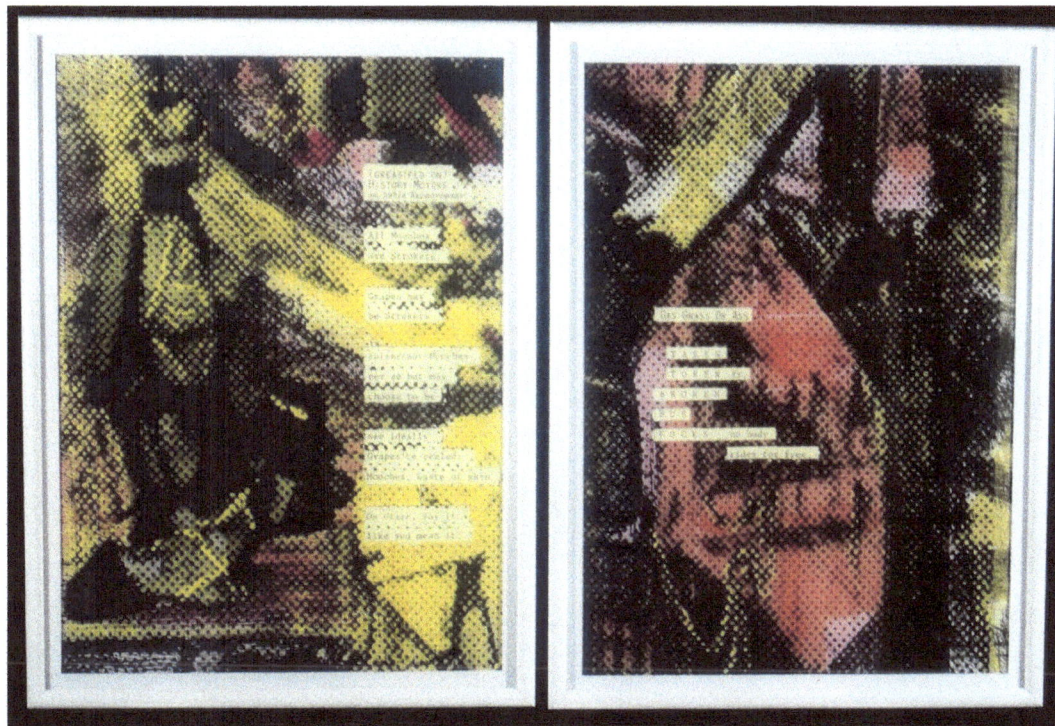

Lustra must've been looking for hours at all my new prints being readied for exhibition, while she loomed overnight for my peepers to pop. By the tone of her *inflection,* she must've last night **wom**aneuvered me a covert introduction to a potent potion—probably at *Rathskeller's* about when I was competing with the juke's *Shaken Baby* metal montage by Moochy Splurgess, "Your name's *Lustra*...as in, '*Lust, Ra!*'"—while a squadron of kamikazes roared themselves down my hatch into *divine wind.* And then—*or was it all really just a weird, loopy dream?*—she grabbed a fistful of manimal while seated right there at the bar pressed up next to me, *Smilin' an' ev'raythang.*

And now I'm here...at home—in my studio...fluttering in from a total eclipse **black out** to a wrench tightening **head band**width of static pixelation.

"Hey, Dickweed," thus spake *"Amrita"* **Amanita,** multi-faceted Indus Goddess, all five faces in my face, "Well for you your tang is all tongueled."

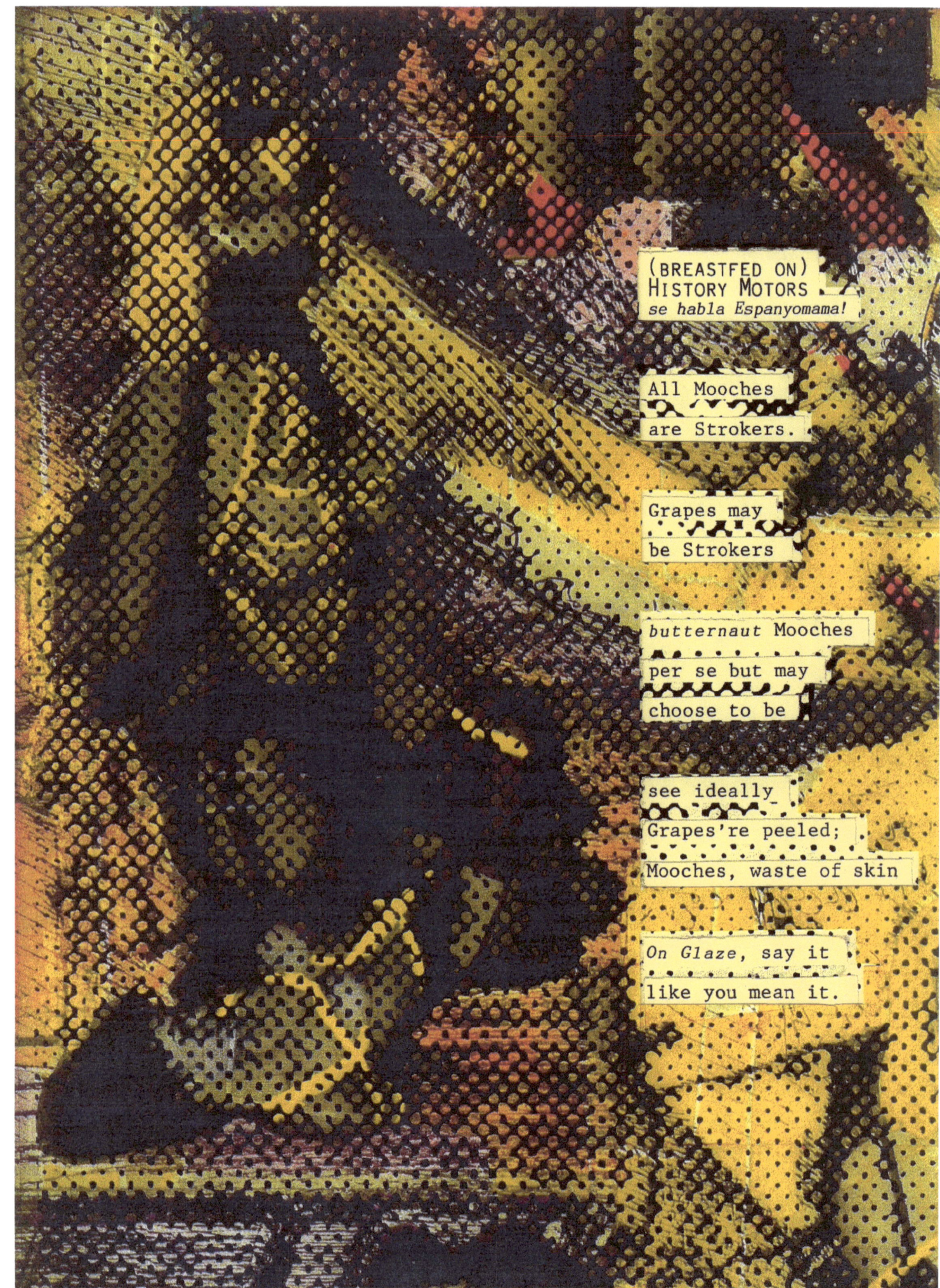

(BREASTFED ON)
HISTORY MOTORS
se habla Espanyomama!

All Mooches
are Strokers.

Grapes may
be Strokers

butternaut Mooches
per se but may
choose to be

see ideally
Grapes're peeled;
Mooches, waste of skin

On Glaze, say it
like you mean it.

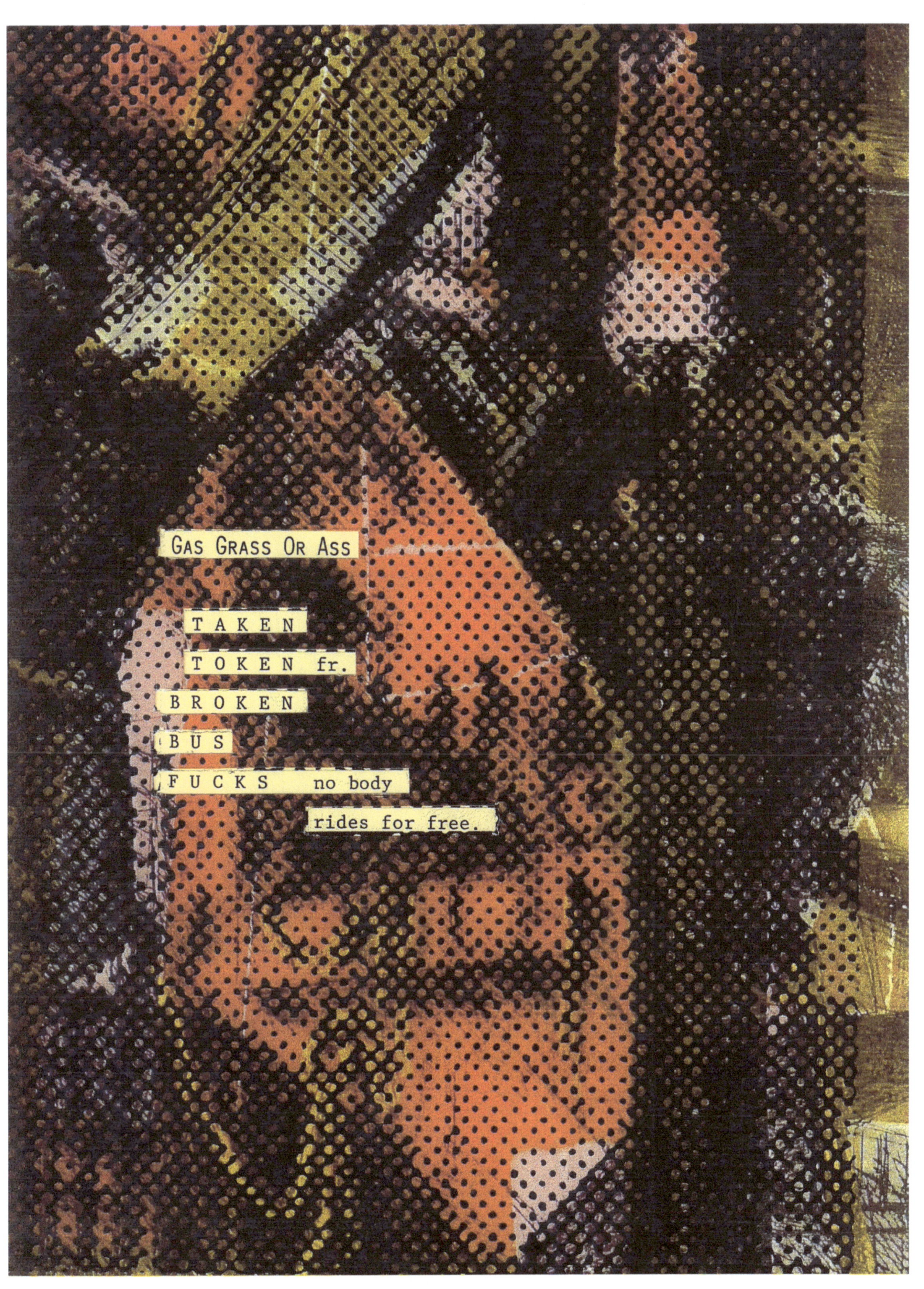

GAS GRASS OR ASS

TAKEN

TOKEN fr.

BROKEN

BUS

FUCKS   no body

rides for free.

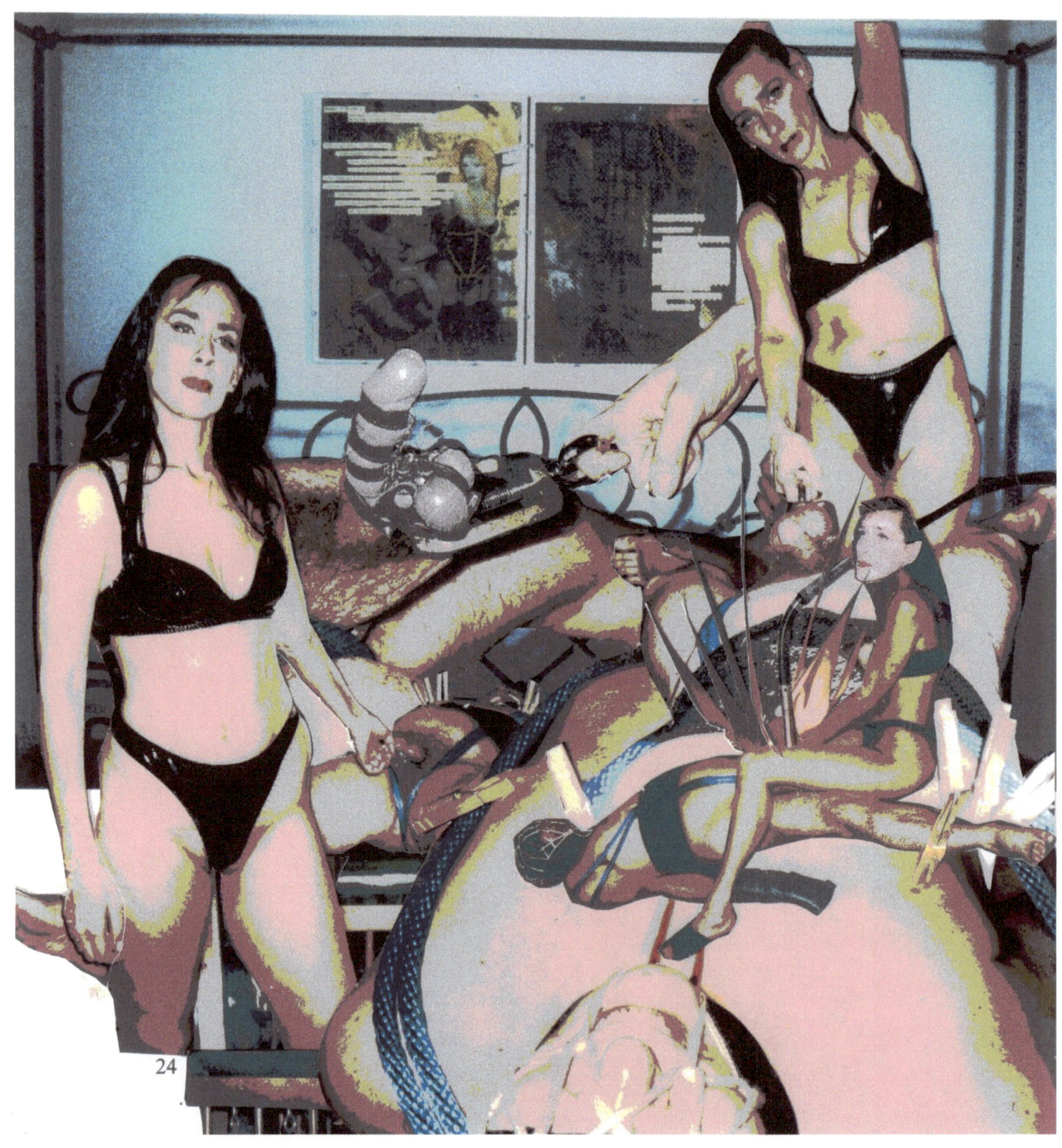

24

Chapter 3
METRO RAIL
Diptych

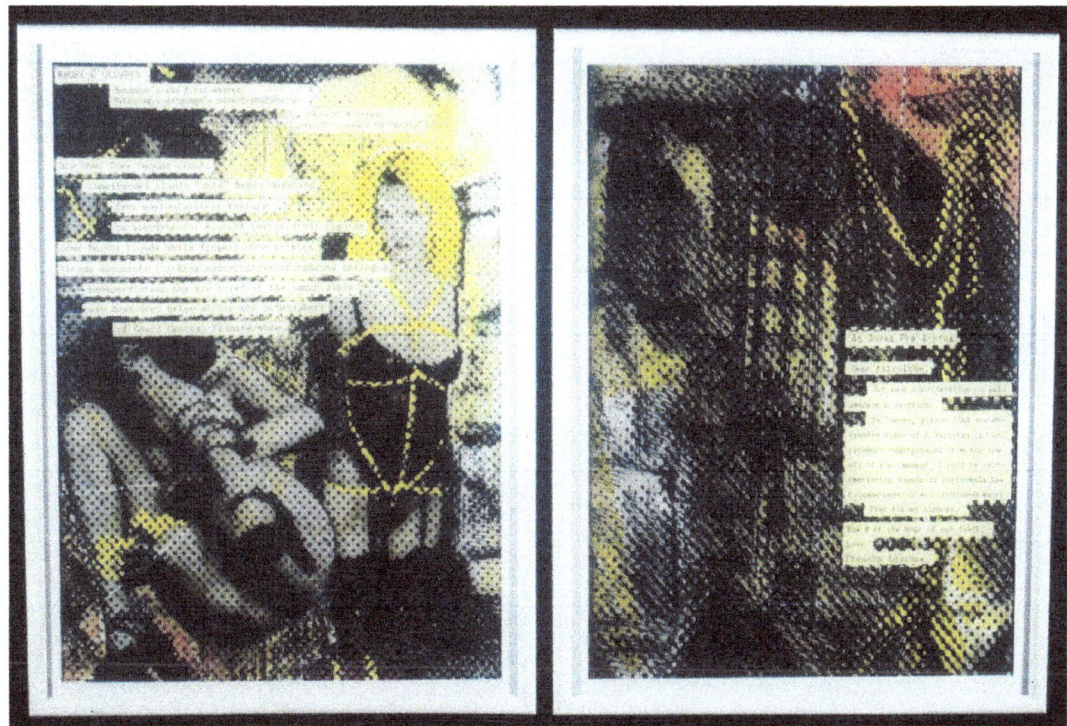

    "You can hear me, Punjabi," Amanita **jab**bed his bread box, "My ambrosia may bind body and gag guile, but you **do** *see* **and**," jab!, "*Hear* me." She was afire, "When I started out we didn't *sneak around* about it. I'd walk right up to a café table, take from my purse and place on the table's edge an empty champagne glass, it's lip at the hemline of my mini, and right in front of the lone, perfectly unprep't gentleman seated *now* not **minding** <u>*his*</u> <u>**own**</u> **business**, dare I say—as well as nearby onlookers, **all** *transfixed*—I would fill up the glass with my elixir from where I stood akimbo, not even having to hike my dress it was so short. Snatched napkin from table; walked.

    "You'd be surprised how many dogs pick up **that** scent, even if they've to run a gauntlet of critics. Sometimes a critic or so would wag along, too.

    "What the alchemists called the 'elixir of life,' the devotional now call 'Midflow with a Twist': The twist?—kidney filtered soma *muscaria* extract."

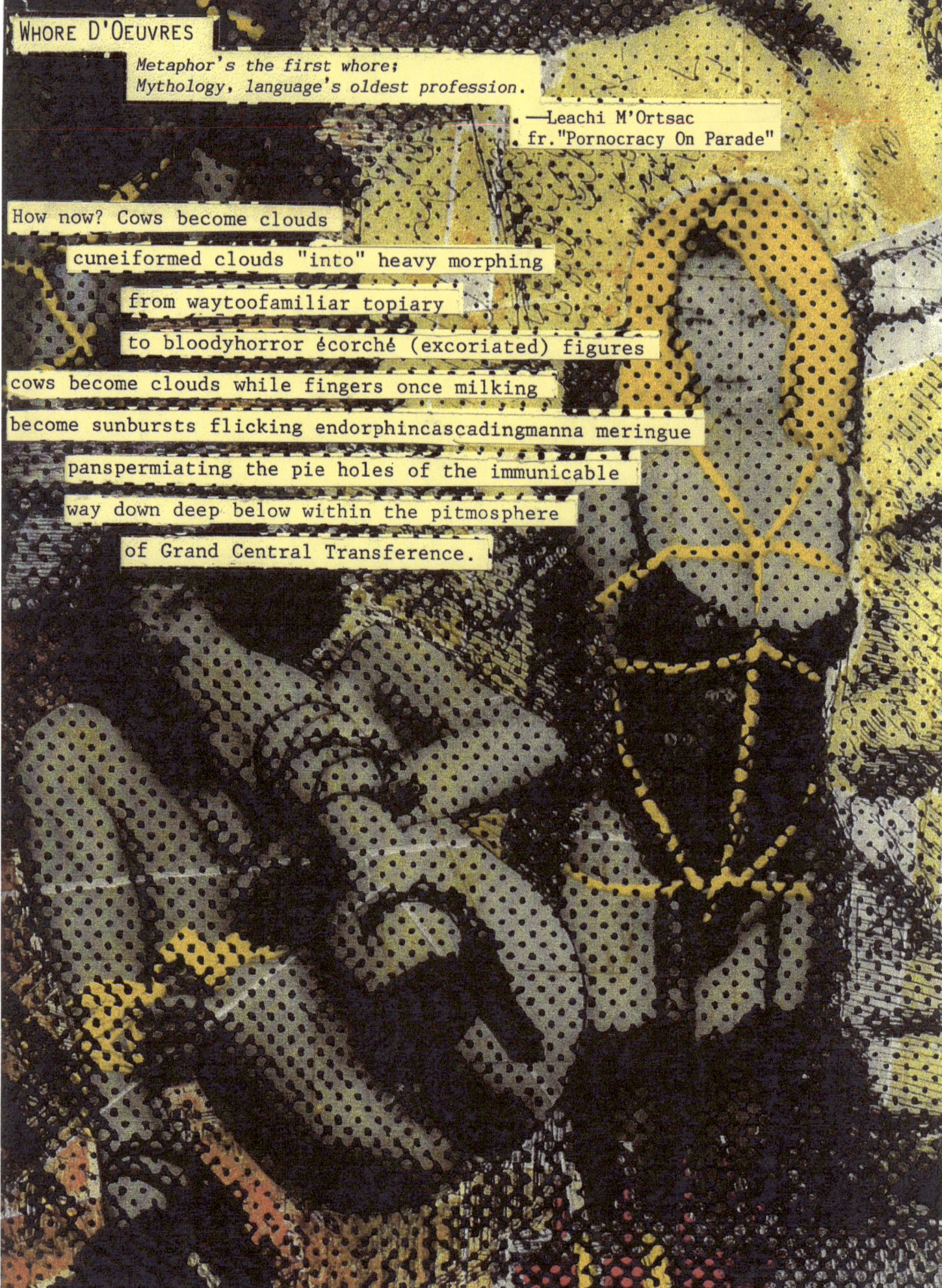

WHORE D'OEUVRES

Metaphor's the first whore;
Mythology, language's oldest profession.

—Leachi M'Ortsac
fr."Pornocracy On Parade"

How now? Cows become clouds

    cuneiformed clouds "into" heavy morphing

    from waytoofamiliar topiary

    to bloodyhorror écorché (excoriated) figures

cows become clouds while fingers once milking

become sunbursts flicking endorphincascadingmanna meringue

panspermiating the pie holes of the immunicable

way down deep below within the pitmosphere

    of Grand Central Transference.

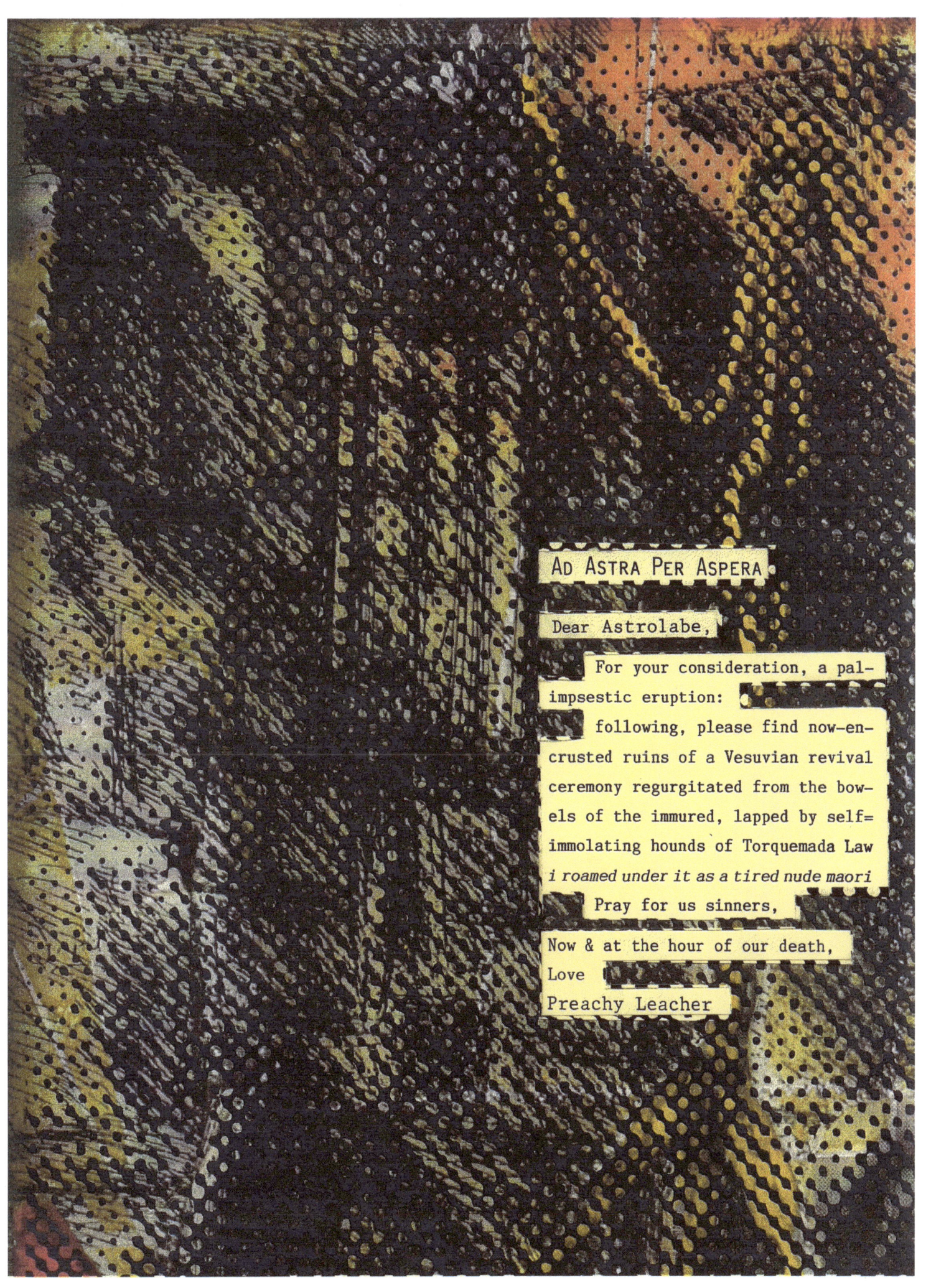

AD ASTRA PER ASPERA

Dear Astrolabe,

For your consideration, a pal-
impsestic eruption:

following, please find now-en-
crusted ruins of a Vesuvian revival
ceremony regurgitated from the bow-
els of the immured, lapped by self=
immolating hounds of Torquemada Law
i roamed under it as a tired nude maori

Pray for us sinners,

Now & at the hour of our death,
Love
Preachy Leacher

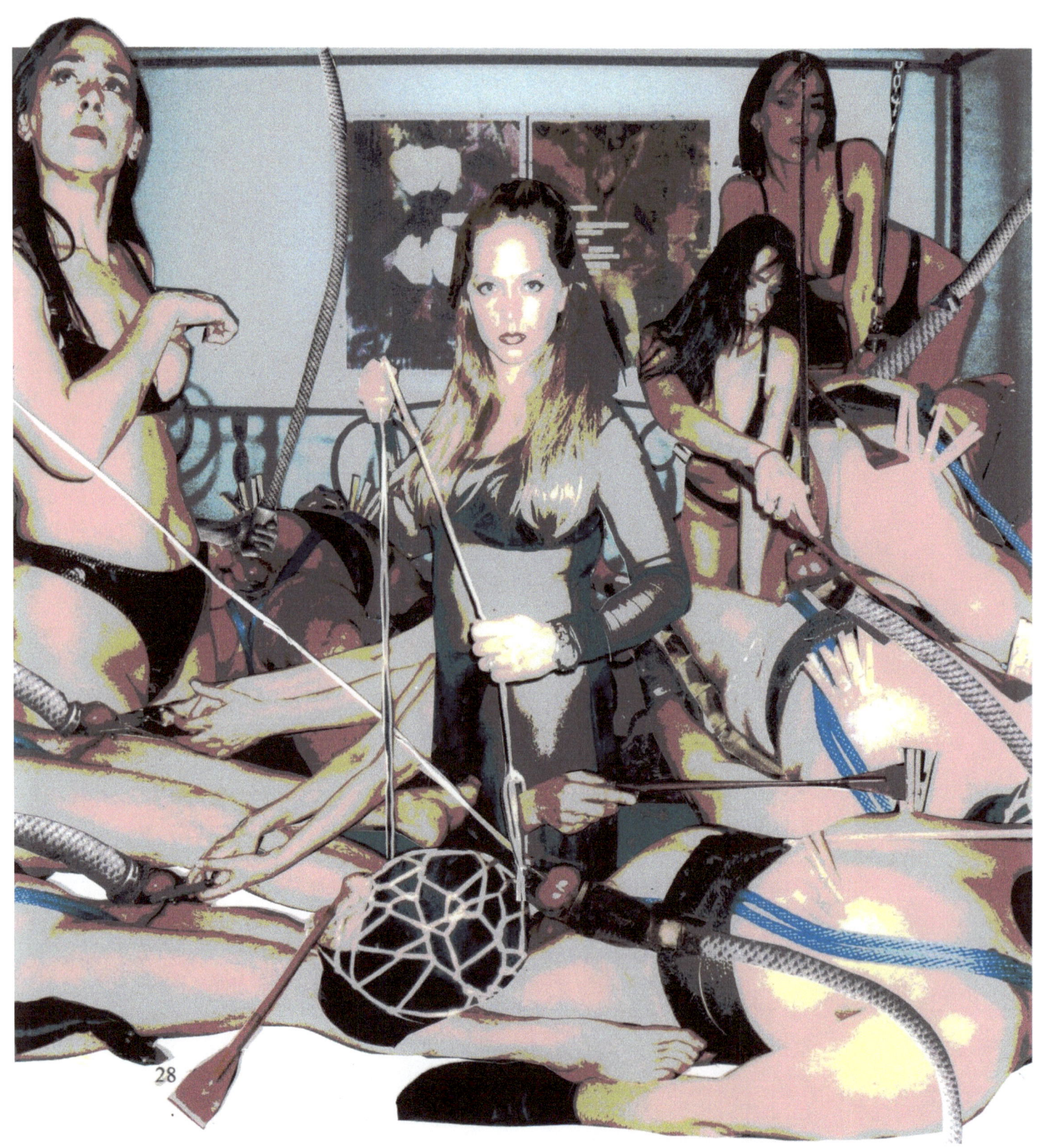

Chapter 4
ASSFAULT
Diptych

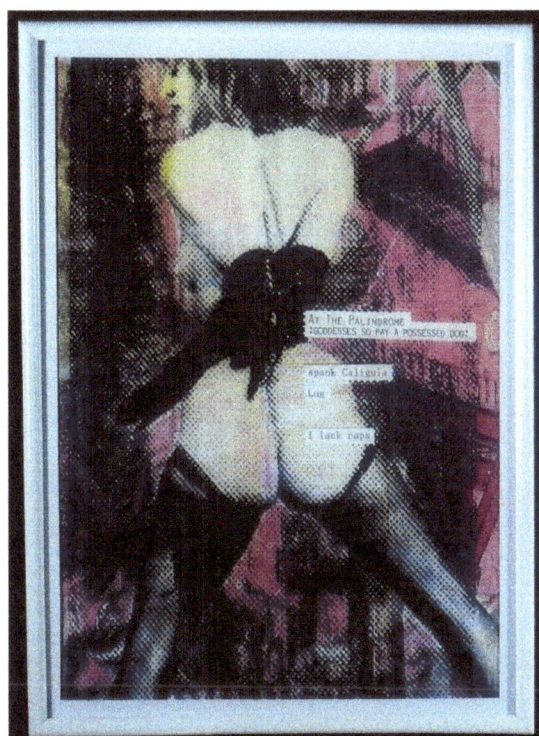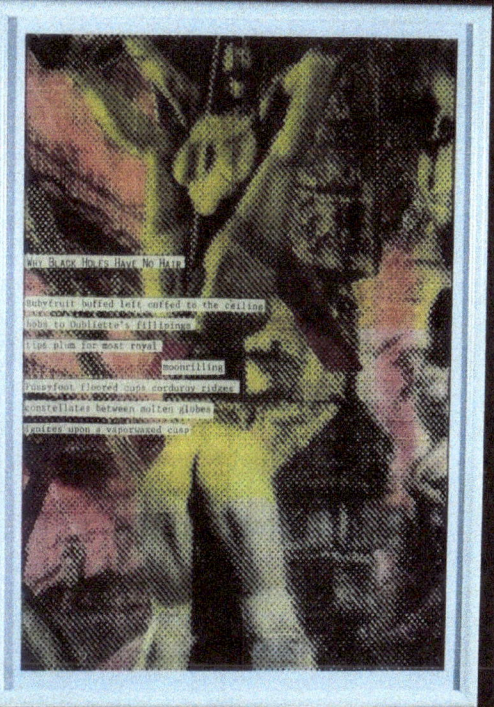

    "But we now prefer to *sneak* **Catherines** down their gullets, don't we, Sister Amrita," *Illustra, save my ass!,* their entangled fly inwardly prayed.

    "I was just reminiscing about sidewalk life in Paris," poofed Amanita—Amrita's her *safe name,* to decrimp her *nom de kink;* yet her inner cauldron bubbled over, "I'm also regaling while draining this piss face of all his color."

    "Patience, *Am',* the roast is better served baked than broiled. His sacrifice must not only be a labor but a transmutation of cream into chrism."

    'Rita swallowed hard, chrism was the coin of the realm, "Love your enthusiasm, tho', kid," then Ms. von Kix leered at the art prints she had hung on all the wall space of the ample studio throughout the night and morning.

    "But the **Catherine**, my dear boy, is a drink named after Catherine the Great of Tzarina Russia—contemporary of Architect Piranesi of *Roma*—she mixed vodka with elixir come *eliquir.* Put a new *twist* on the **Enlightenment.**"

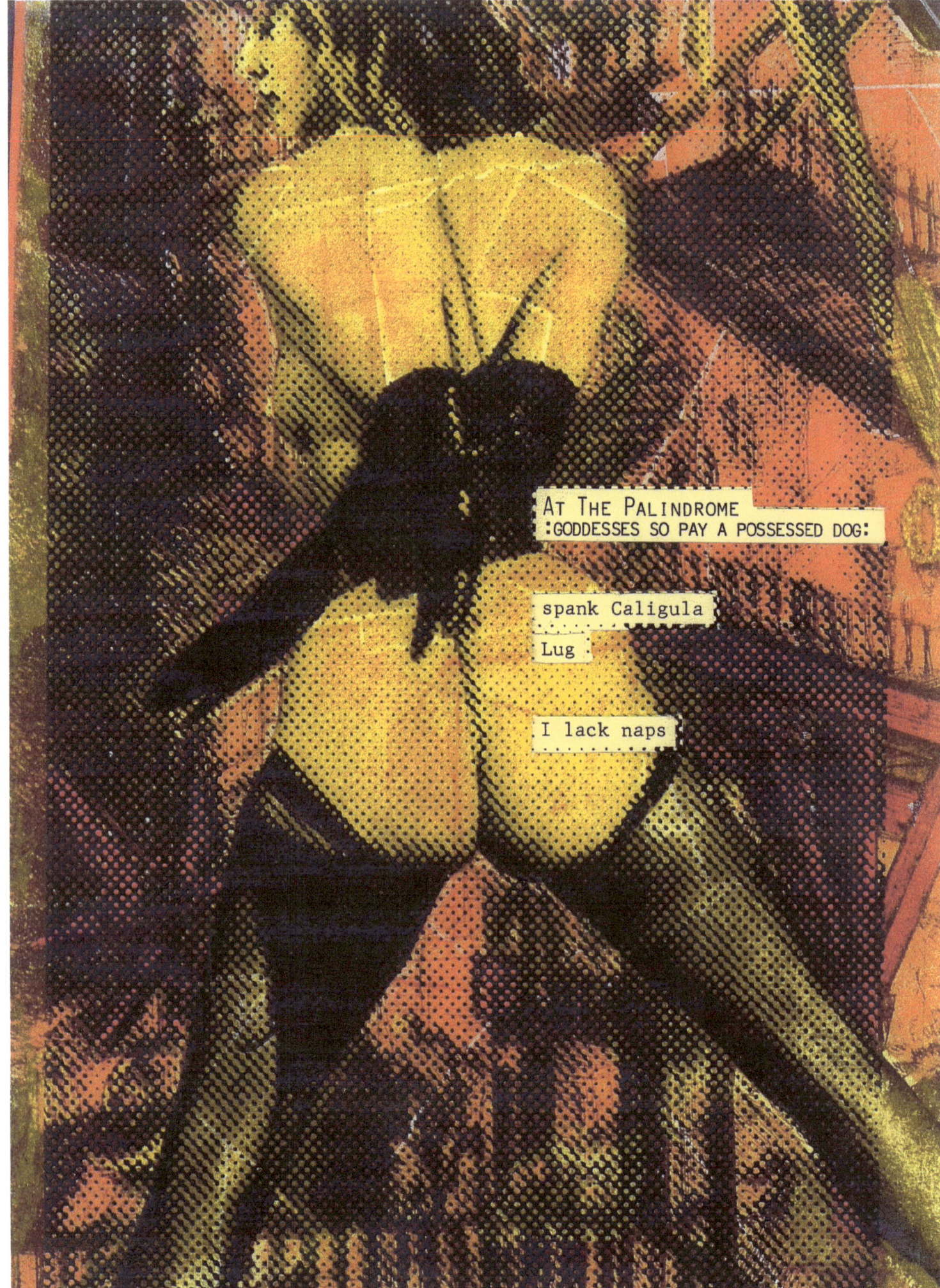

At The Palindrome
:GODDESSES SO PAY A POSSESSED DOG:

spank Caligula

Lug

I lack naps

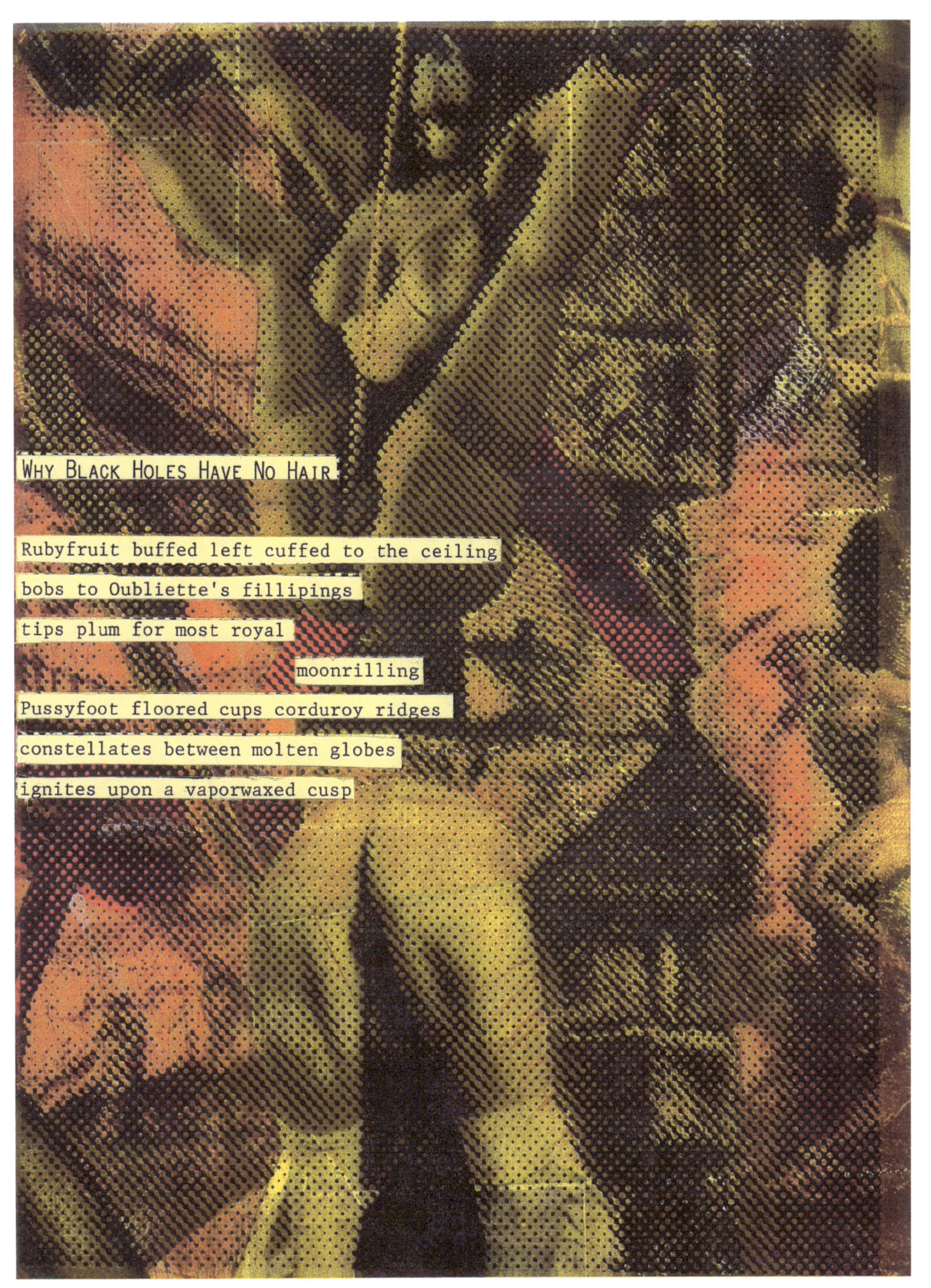

WHY BLACK HOLES HAVE NO HAIR

Rubyfruit buffed left cuffed to the ceiling

bobs to Oubliette's fillipings

tips plum for most royal

                    moonrilling

Pussyfoot floored cups corduroy ridges

constellates between molten globes

ignites upon a vaporwaxed cusp

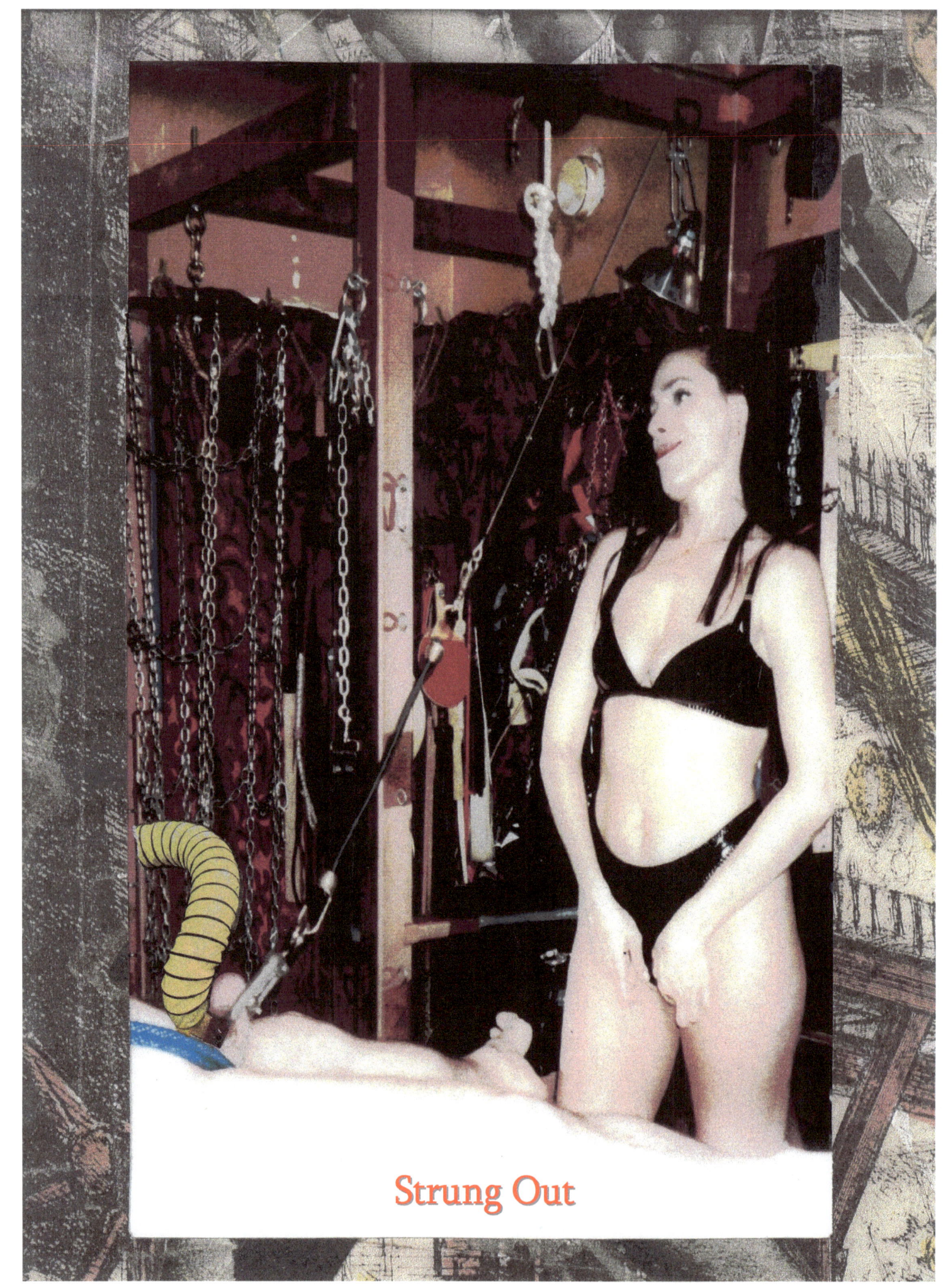

Strung Out

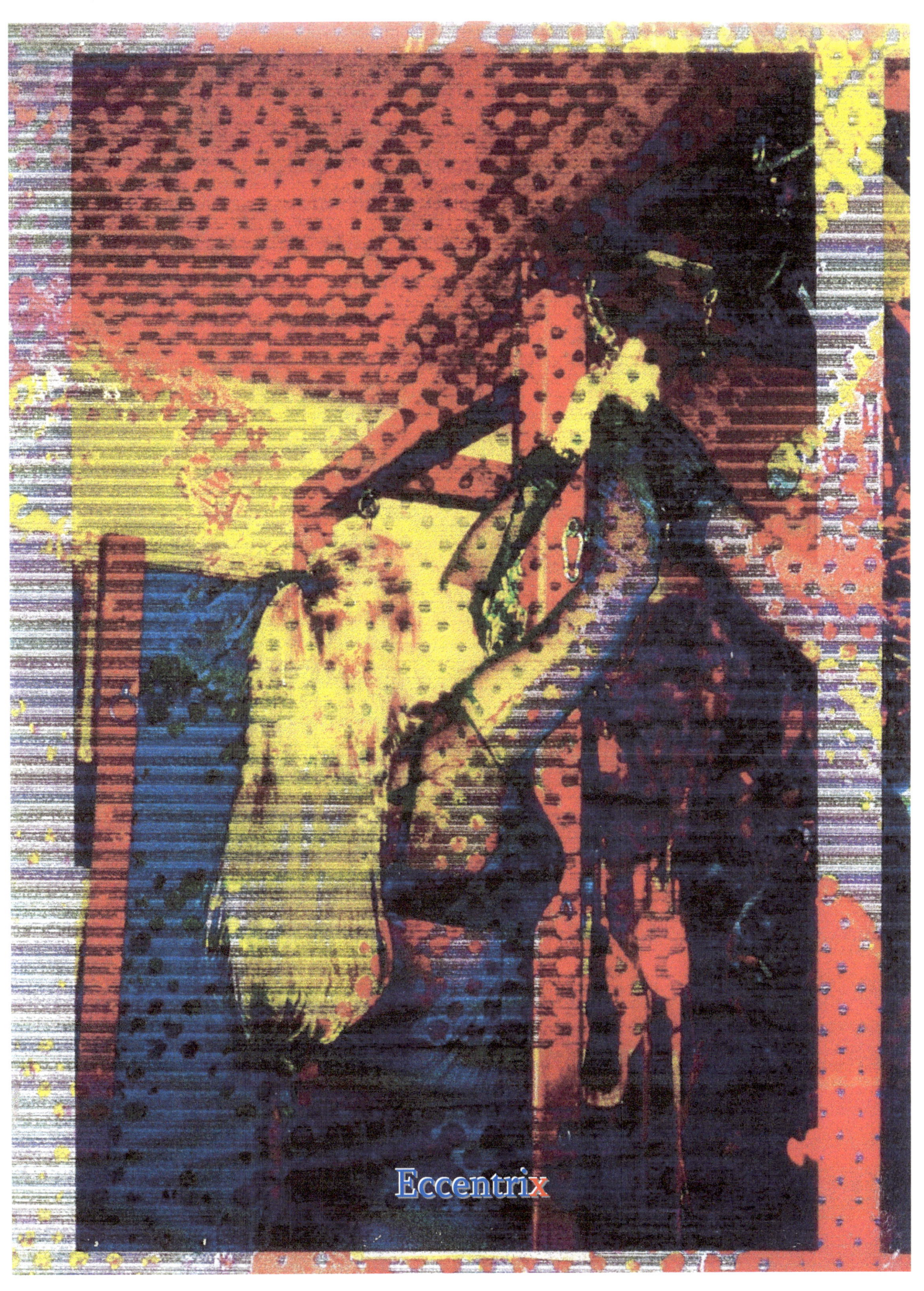
Eccentrix

Phoenix in Effigy

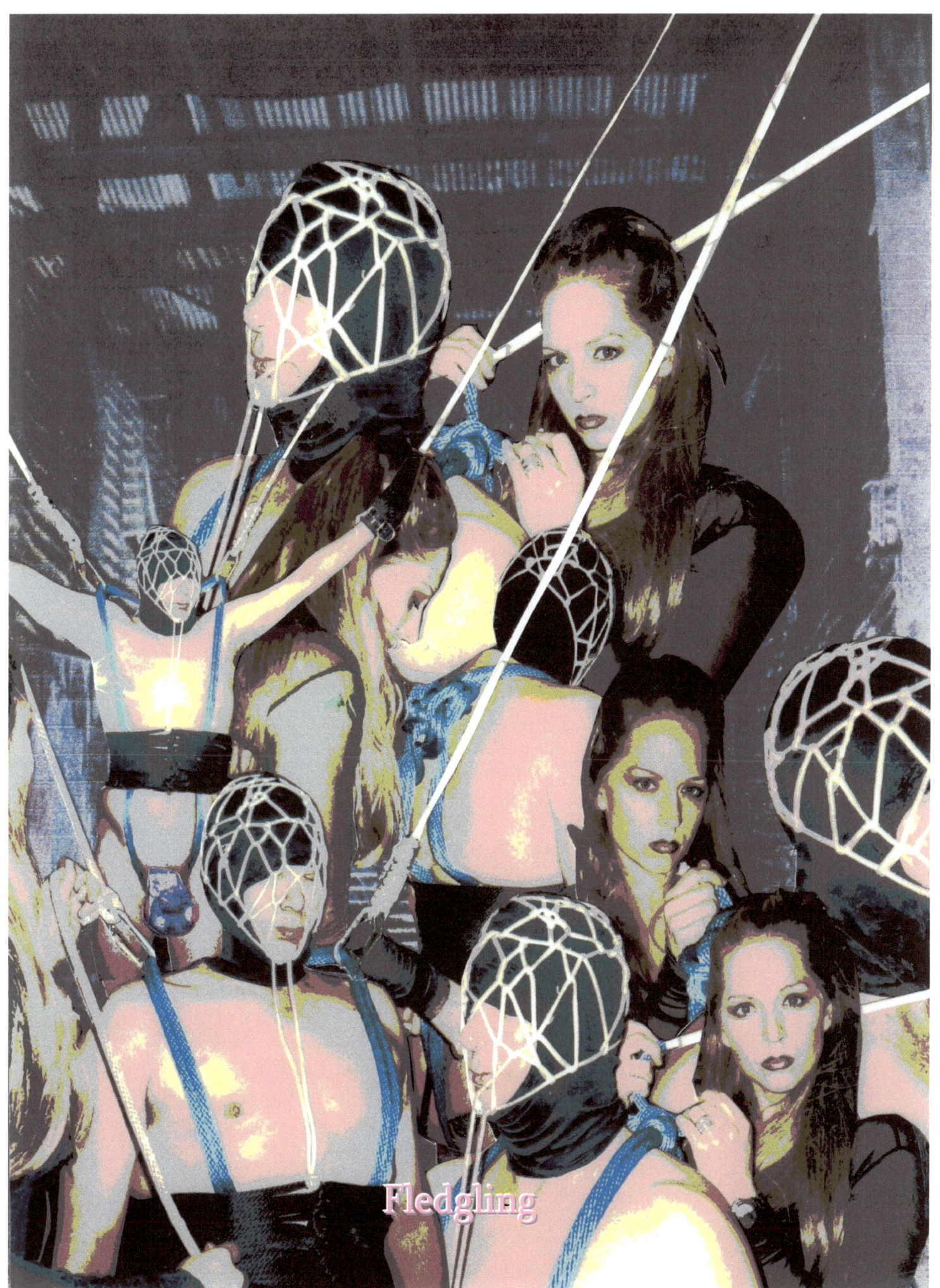

Fledgling

Chapter 5
PURPLE PIRANESI
Pentaptych

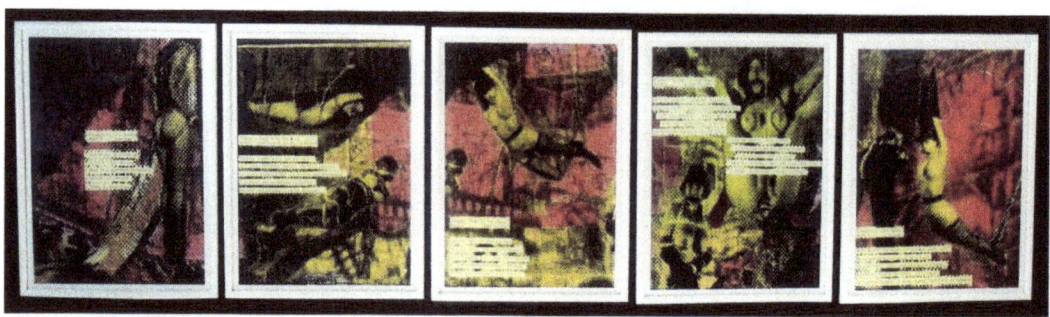

To: **Ms. Diz,**

     My E-rides through your Magic Queendom make me feel so delivered from the shadow of the Valley of Ennui.

     I confess I dream your kiss is the Breath of Life Itself. Can a man remain tethered to the earth after such a gift?

     My dear Illustra, don't you just love dreaming you're flying? Me, too; better pinch me,

Fr: **Micycle.**

To: **oppoet,**

     Yum!m!m!m!m!

     This qualifies for letter of the week ! ! !

     I may have to whore you out again – beware!

     I would LOVE to pinch you!

Fr: **Lustra.**

     Needless to say, the Tantrixhood no longer had to police him. The Nidus Plexus routed his thoughts—deliberate *or* whimsical—to his controller, his *Creatrix.* And she, in turn, would book his render unto Seizor Central.

     And so, as per "Dialog Sheet," she has called her creature forth. Tonight's command performance: Sir Render delivers himself to the Umbiliphiliatrix, Shaydee von Shockra, to her 'Lectric Lair of Horrors where his glist gets blistered to a bitchen gloss, **"no holes barred."**

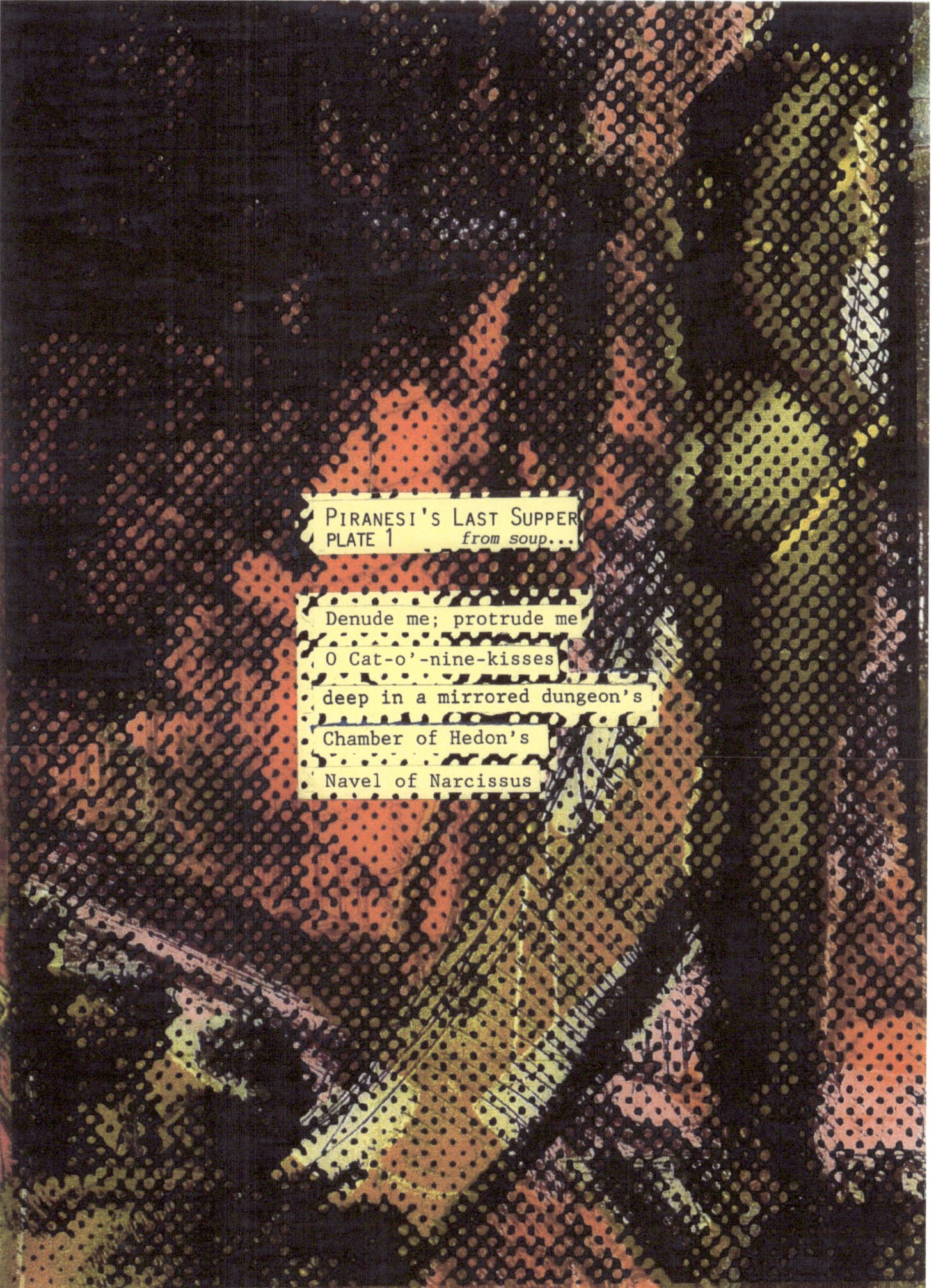

PIRANESI'S LAST SUPPER
PLATE 1   *from soup...*

Denude me; protrude me

O Cat-o'-nine-kisses

deep in a mirrored dungeon's

Chamber of Hedon's

Navel of Narcissus

PIRANESI SHEETS TO THE WIND
PLATE 2 *salad days in The Hanging Gardens*

cinched - winched - and pinched -

all fours strapped towards the four posters .

of a cat's-cradle bed all scaffolded and webbed

harnessed and suspended leviathan

hoisted and dropped - belly flopped -

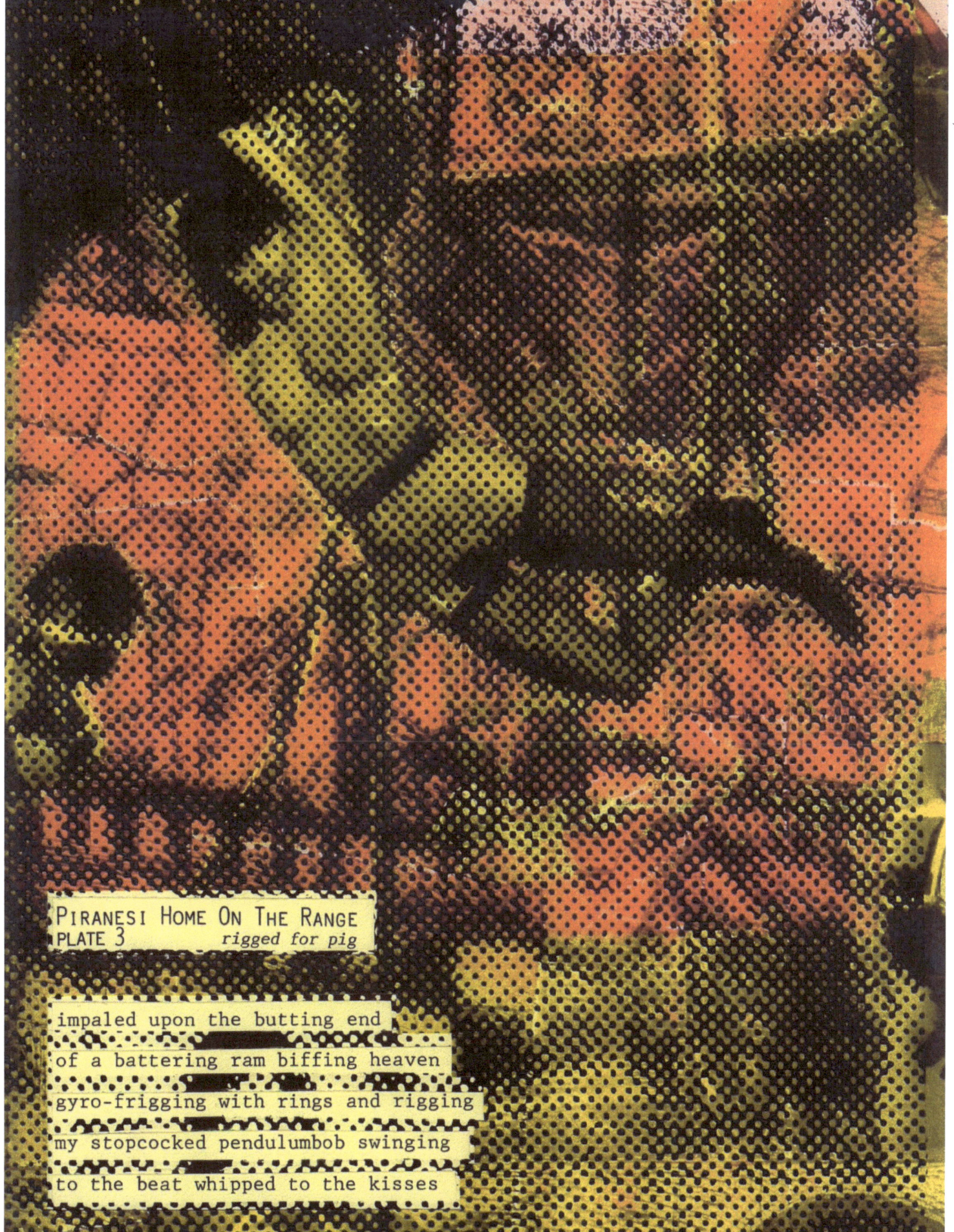

PIRANESI HOME ON THE RANGE
PLATE 3   *rigged for pig*

impaled upon the butting end
of a battering ram biffing heaven
gyro-frigging with rings and rigging
my stopcocked pendulumbob swinging
to the beat whipped to the kisses

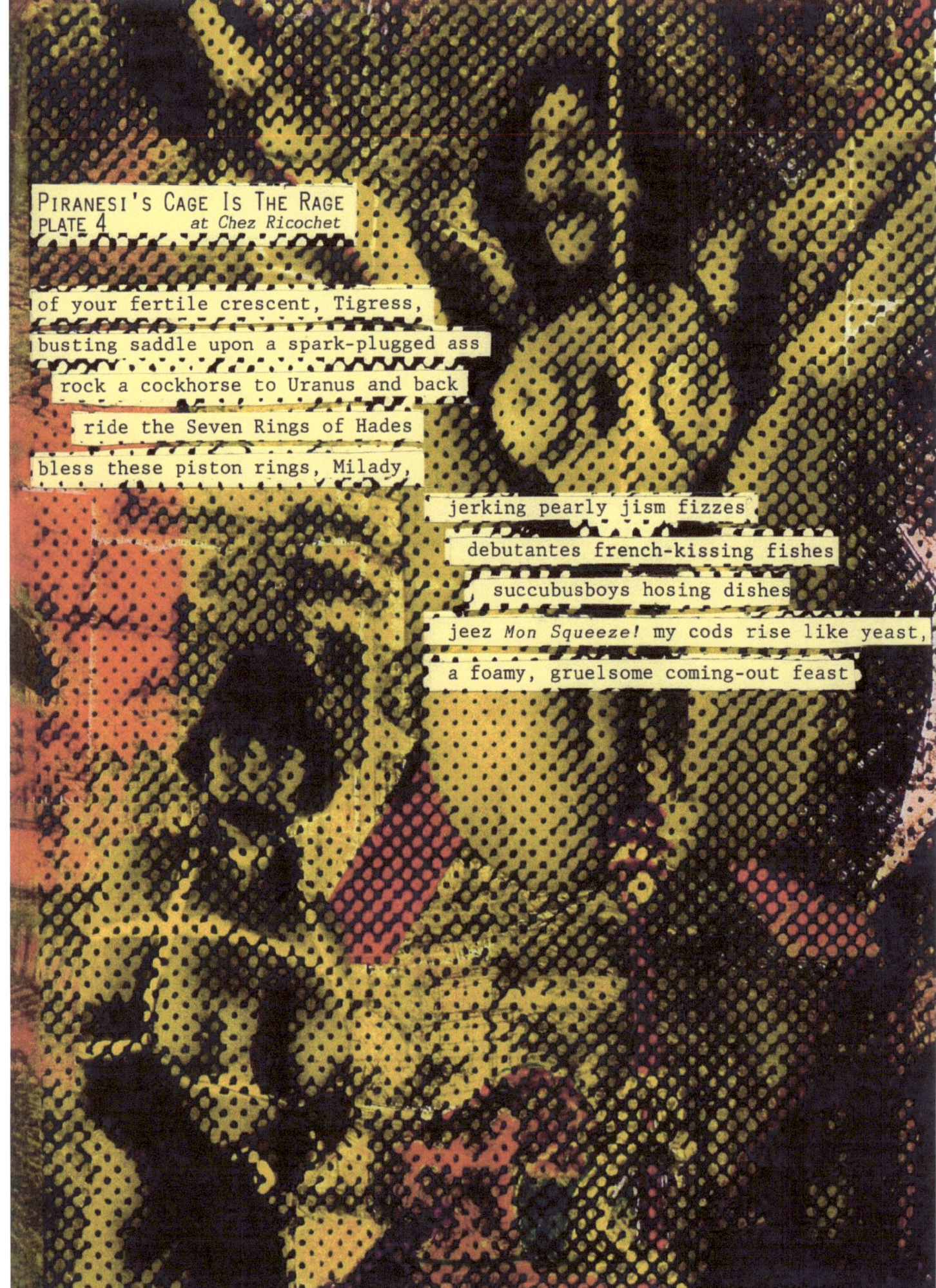

PIRANESI'S CAGE IS THE RAGE
PLATE 4   *at Chez Ricochet*

of your fertile crescent, Tigress,

busting saddle upon a spark-plugged ass

rock a cockhorse to Uranus and back

ride the Seven Rings of Hades

bless these piston rings, Milady,

jerking pearly jism fizzes

debutantes french-kissing fishes

succubusboys hosing dishes

jeez *Mon Squeeze!* my cods rise like yeast,

a foamy, gruelsome coming-out feast

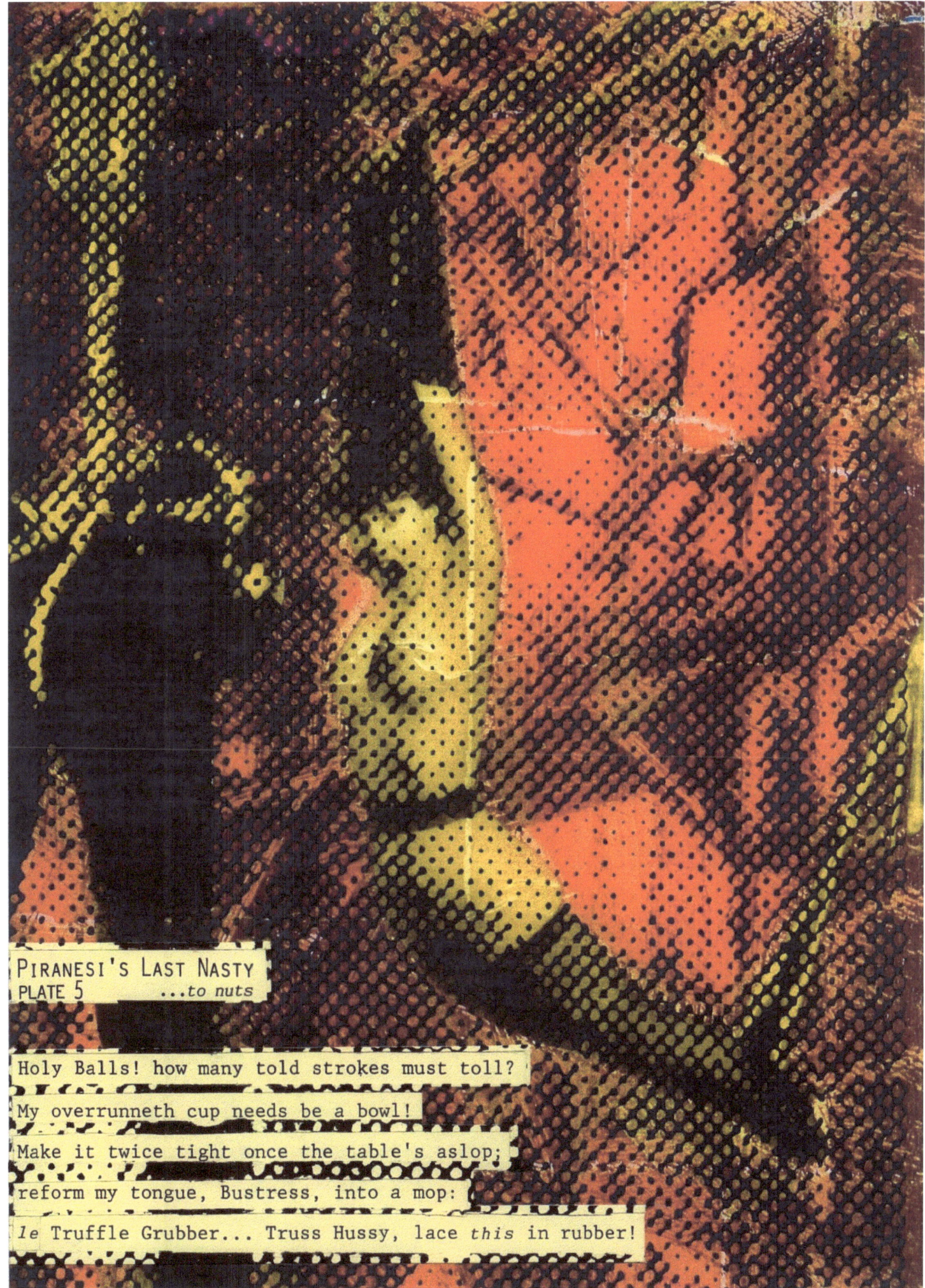

PIRANESI'S LAST NASTY
PLATE 5   ...to nuts

Holy Balls! how many told strokes must toll?

My overrunneth cup needs be a bowl!

Make it twice tight once the table's aslop;

reform my tongue, Bustress, into a mop:

le Truffle Grubber... Truss Hussy, lace *this* in rubber!

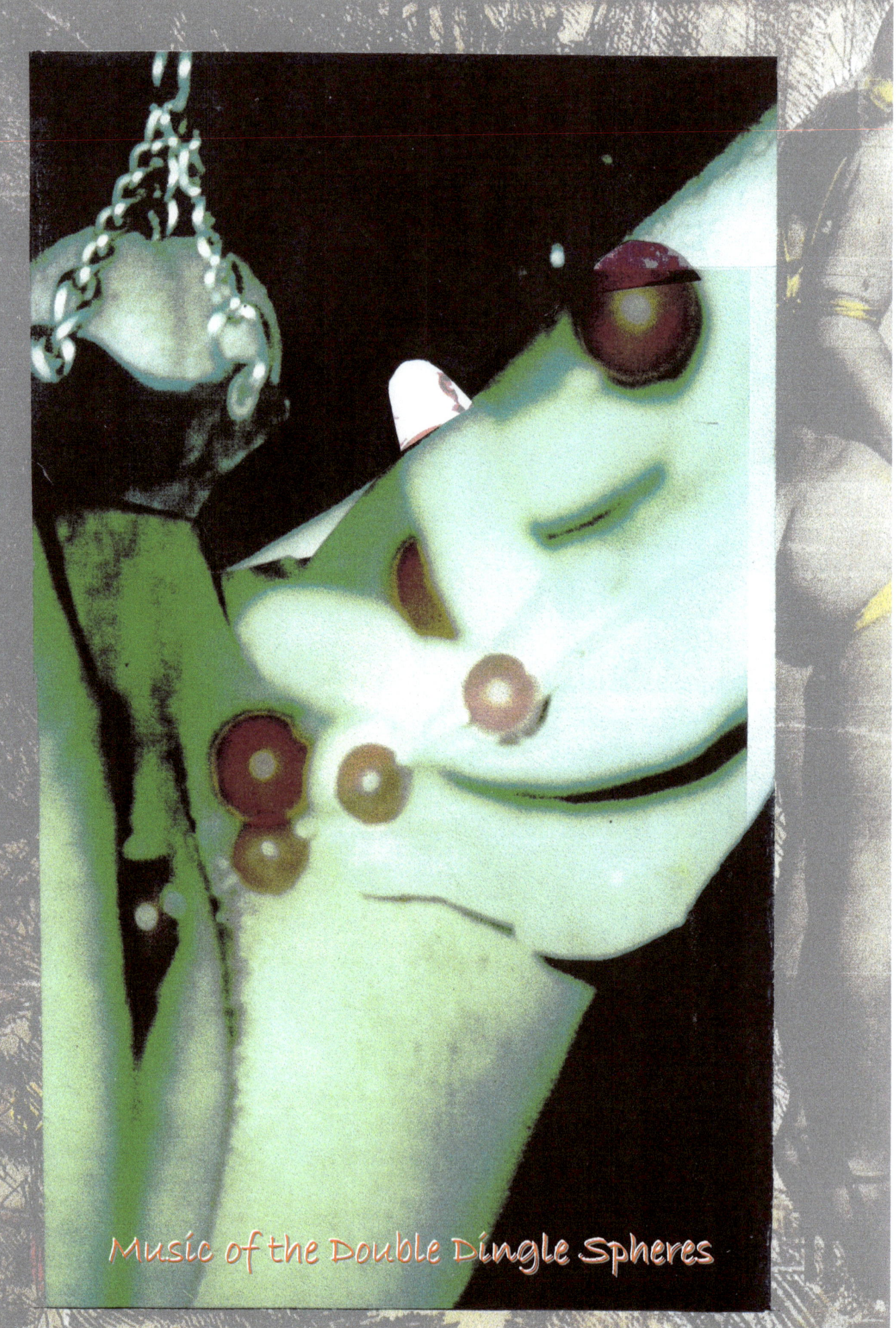

Music of the Double Dingle Spheres

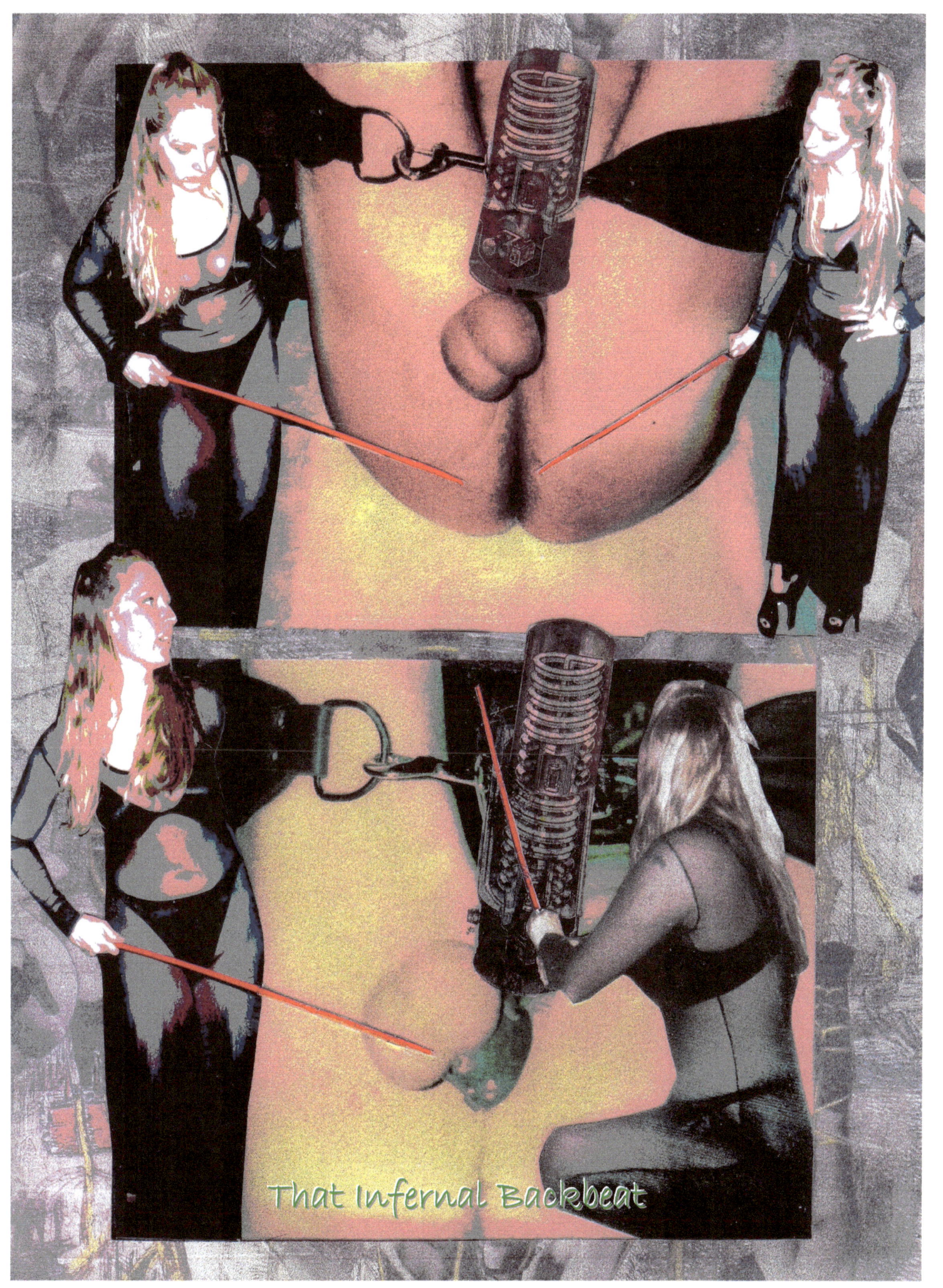

That Infernal Backbeat

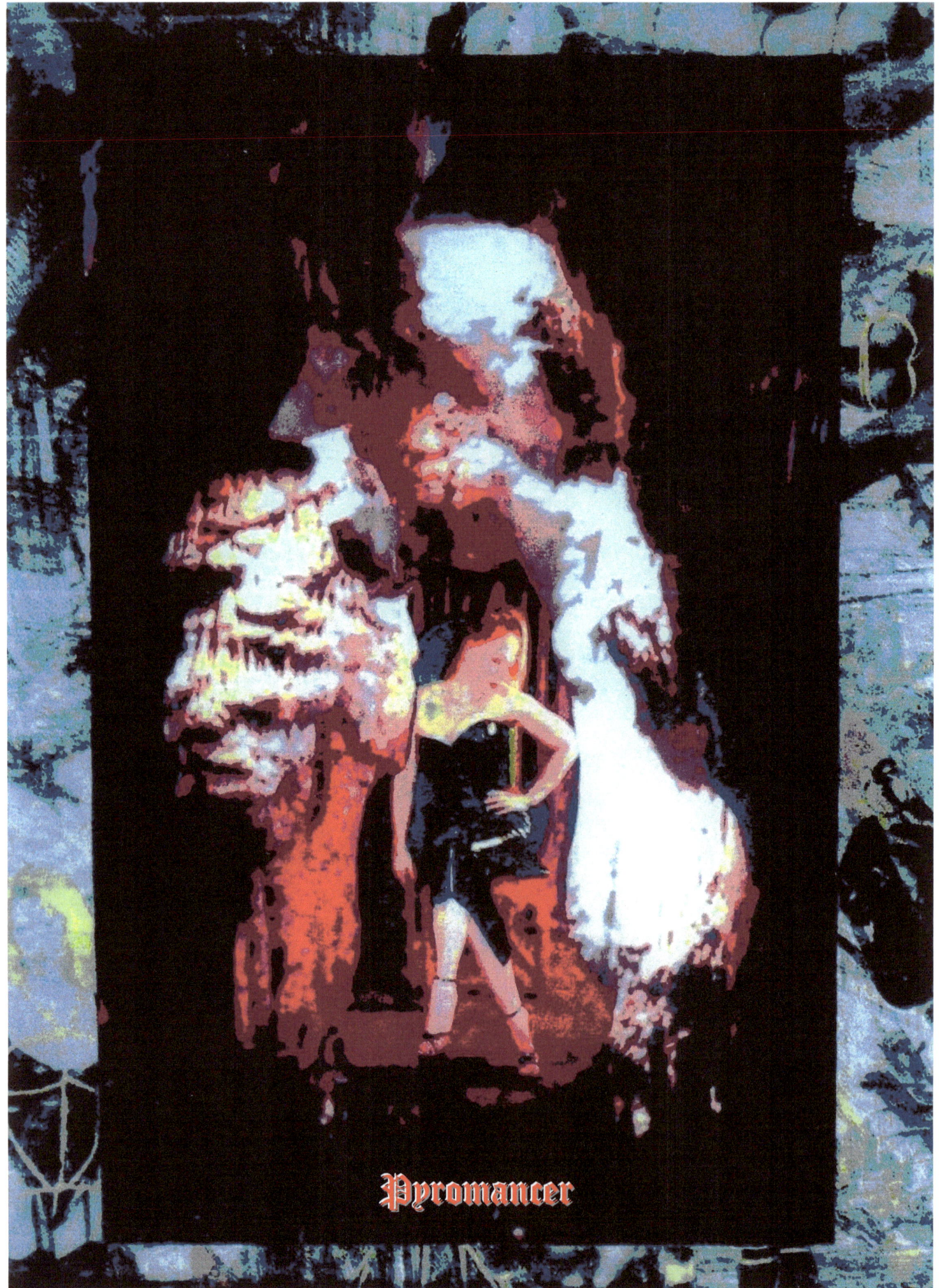

Chapter 6
ARACHNOPTYCH
Sextuptych

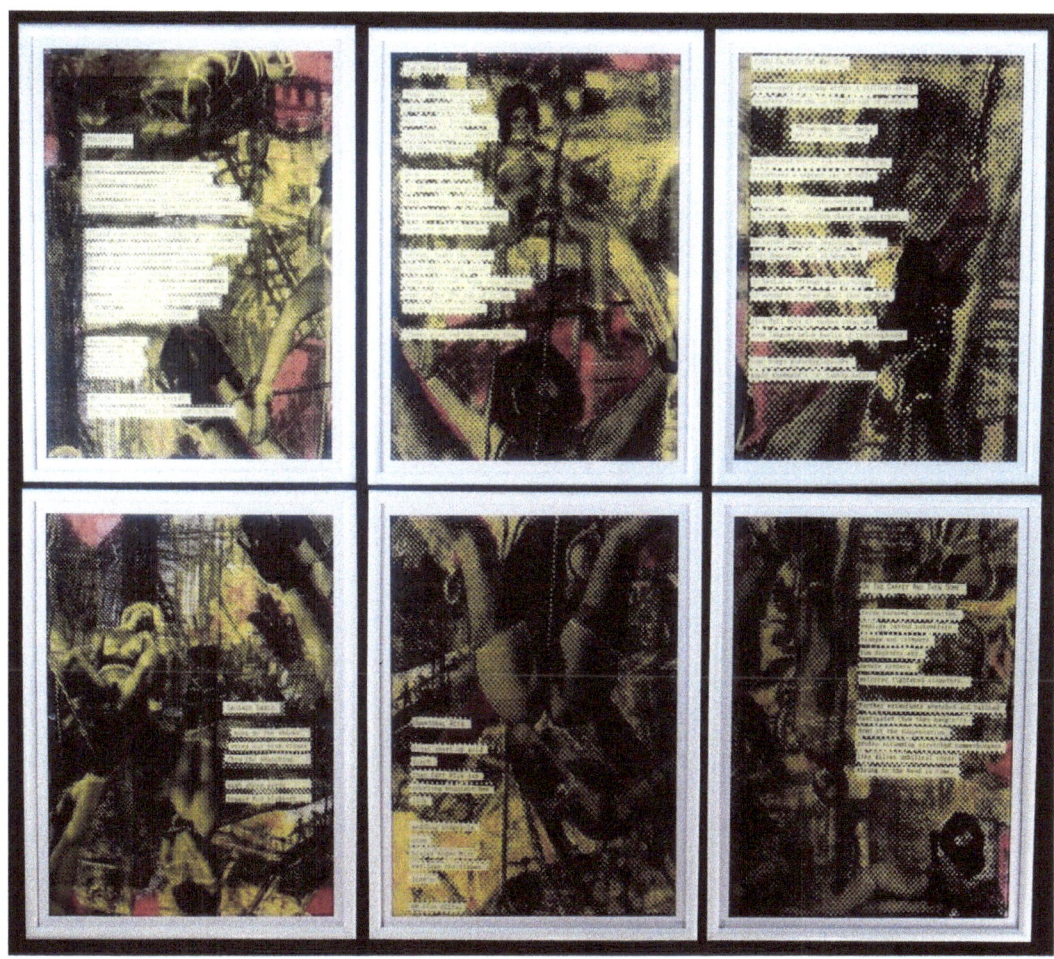

born: Lost in the Labyrinth from mentally cataloging its infernal puzzles until overwhelmed, I then relied on fortune to meander my way out as if my enmazement were not a sentence but a freedom. Not until my wit was spent did my circummuration go peristaltic. Near exhaustion, at the threshold of panic, I spotted, then desperately squeezed through a shuttering portal to abort in an amniotic sweat, damning my fickle flesh for escaping from a well earned, eternal fumbling at the Gordian slipknot that held me in suspense.

died: *Fancy Trim,* read the sign over the Factory Street door. *I'll **jes'** bet.*

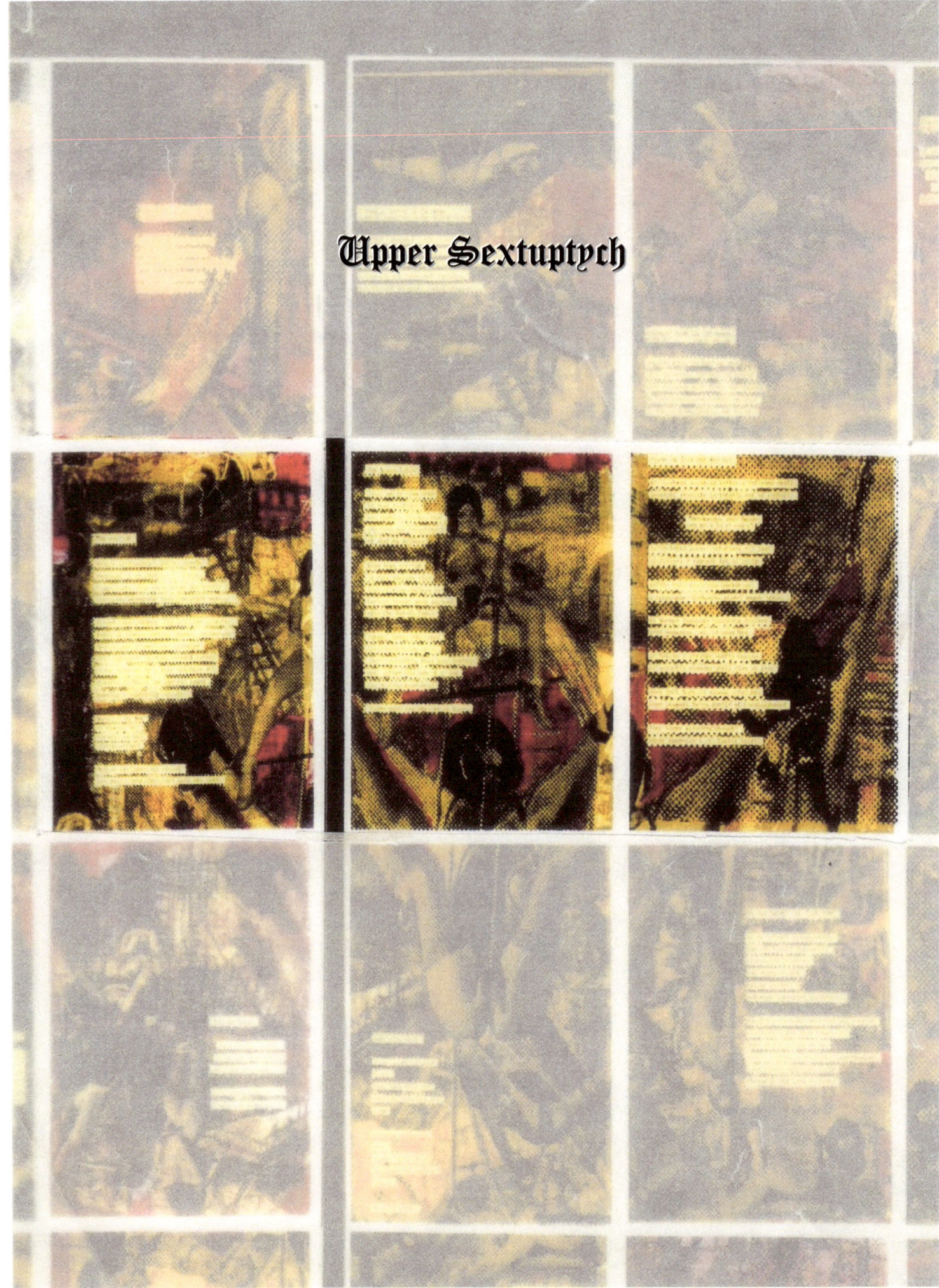

Upper Sextuptych

MOXIBUSTION

Within Schizandra's gutted temple
Whooping up an exorcist's circle
Flagellants gird their loins for Battle
Berserko: Weregoths blow the house down...

Singed rope-ladders, lop-pulleyed catwalks,
Bulks of timber jutting skewed, splintered
Mostly into pickets yet somewise
This ruptured, listing lookout turret
Stays tethered by a fine cunthair yet
Tarotia fishnets the sky for signs
Humming a lumbering lullaby:

Warden o' The Way
or wayward, ho!
how will you log,
Crystal or Coal?

Mobile testimonials reveal
The Deal: fold this hand into the next.

THE NIDUS TOUCH

Tyra, we'll have none
of your tantrums
nor tantric tricks, nun
(or have you forgotten?)
of deus ex machina

know your station
in this passion play
dear or else confess in
forlorn truant ward splayed
upon the Woe-oh Cross

intern, learn the ropes
doped with sappy attar
young succulent, know your betters
must suffer the rub of it but
lac it song gnostical

'tween piss and shit we're born.

YOUTH IN ASIA ONE WAY OUT

Ric-o-chets a-cubing within a pillowed skull
monsters from the id totally out of control:

"Telemoroñes, Señor Omelet
you got a lot o' *huevos"*

infibulated portal unbuttons its lips
spitshines a sapient sac of jelly

shifts into psilocyberoverdrive:
a telescape—forbidden planet wagon train.

Be warned lemmings beginning descent
into dementia, all of whom bed

in bedlam a strange ventriloquism
of acoustic shadows shall rise up from

then fall back to sunken catacombs
some leagues below knells of tromlongboned

sump pumps gosuckyglubsucky
squid squeezin's 'n' turnip hairs.

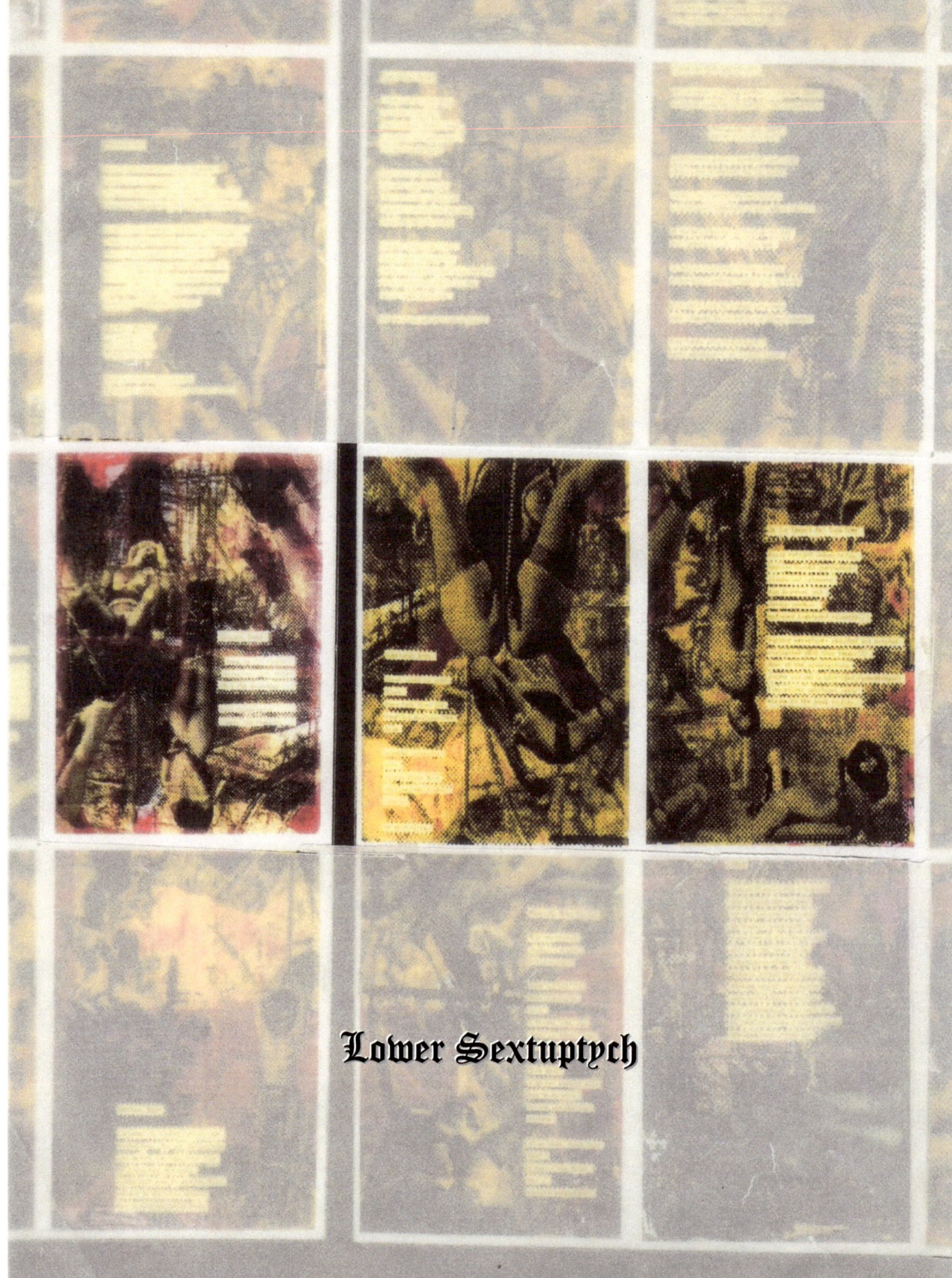

Lower Sextuptych

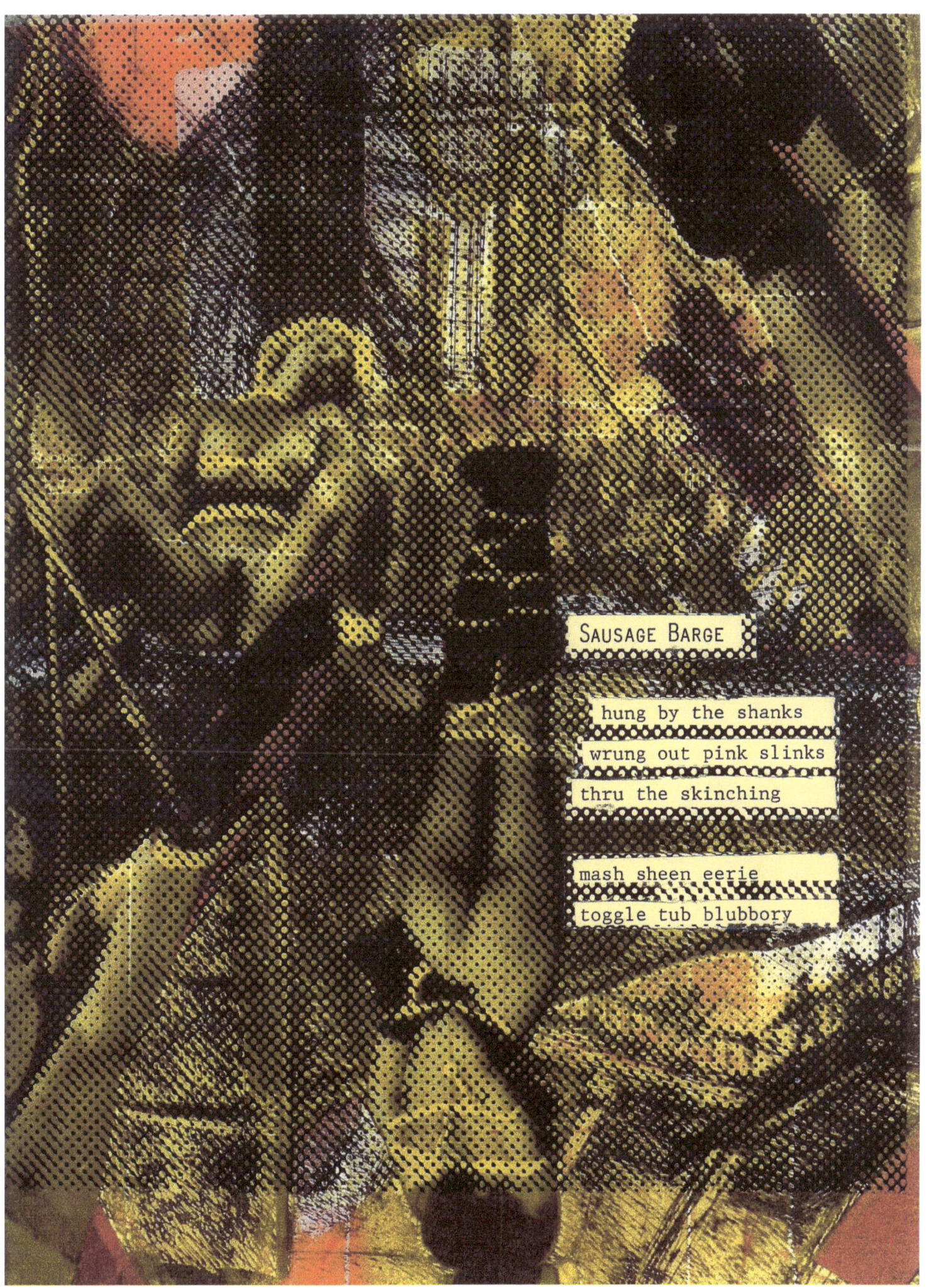

Sausage Barge

hung by the shanks
wrung out pink slinks
thru the skinching

mash sheen eerie
toggle tub blubbory

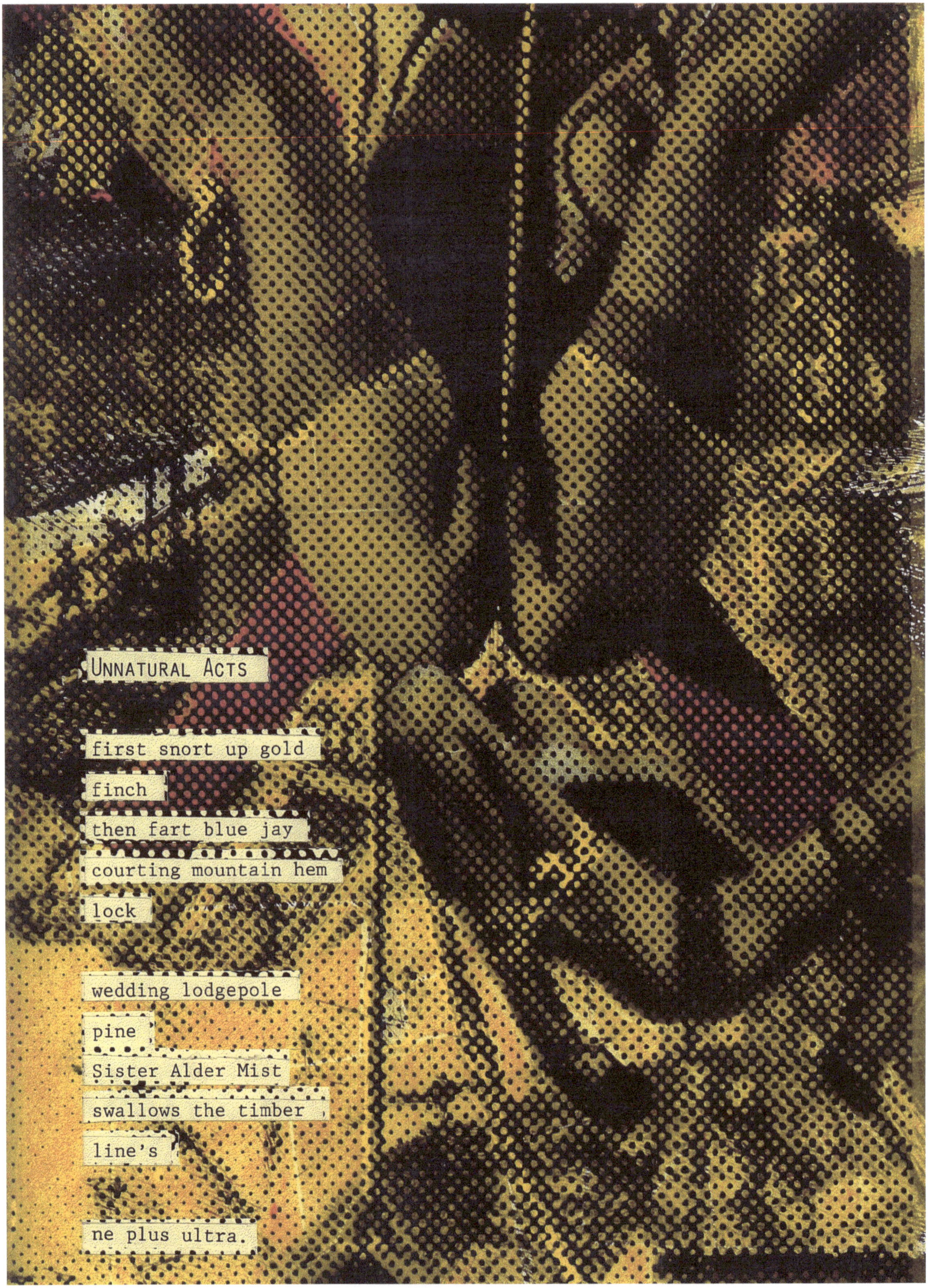

Unnatural Acts

first snort up gold

finch

then fart blue jay

courting mountain hem

lock

wedding lodgepole

pine

Sister Alder Mist

swallows the timber

line's

ne plus ultra.

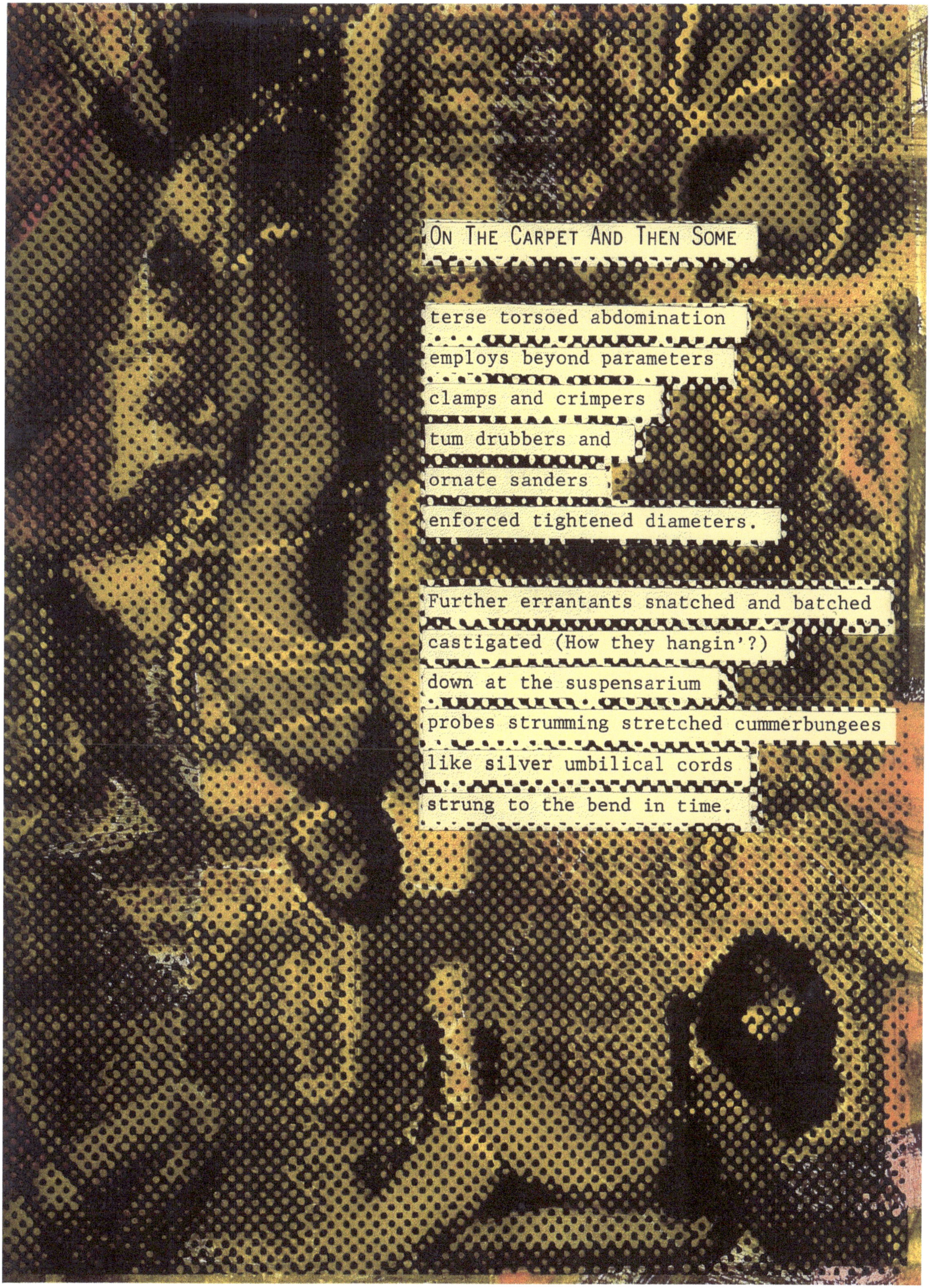

On The Carpet And Then Some

terse torsoed abdomination
employs beyond parameters
clamps and crimpers
tum drubbers and
ornate sanders
enforced tightened diameters.

Further errantants snatched and batched
castigated (How they hangin'?)
down at the suspensarium
probes strumming stretched cummerbungees
like silver umbilical cords
strung to the bend in time.

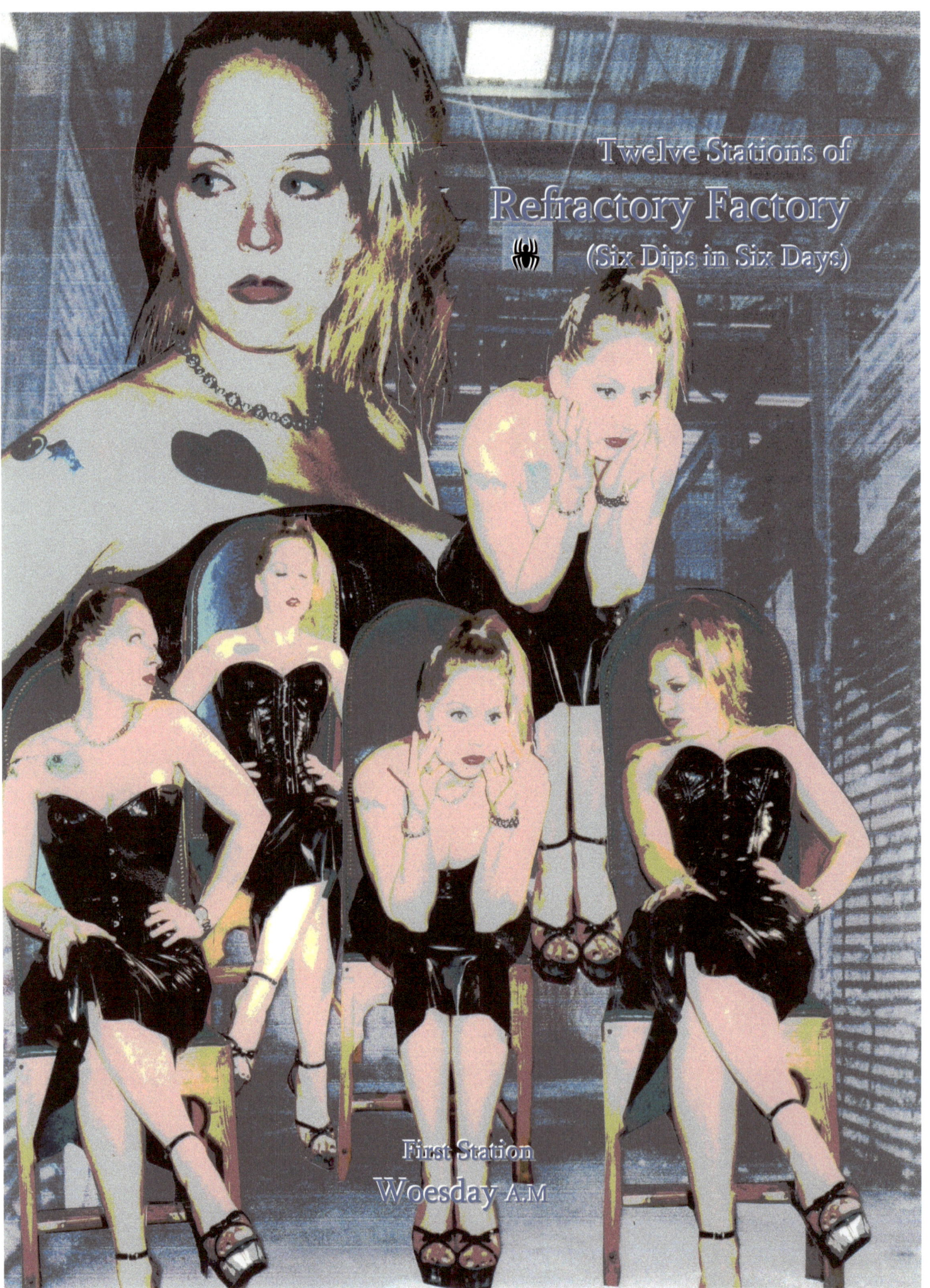

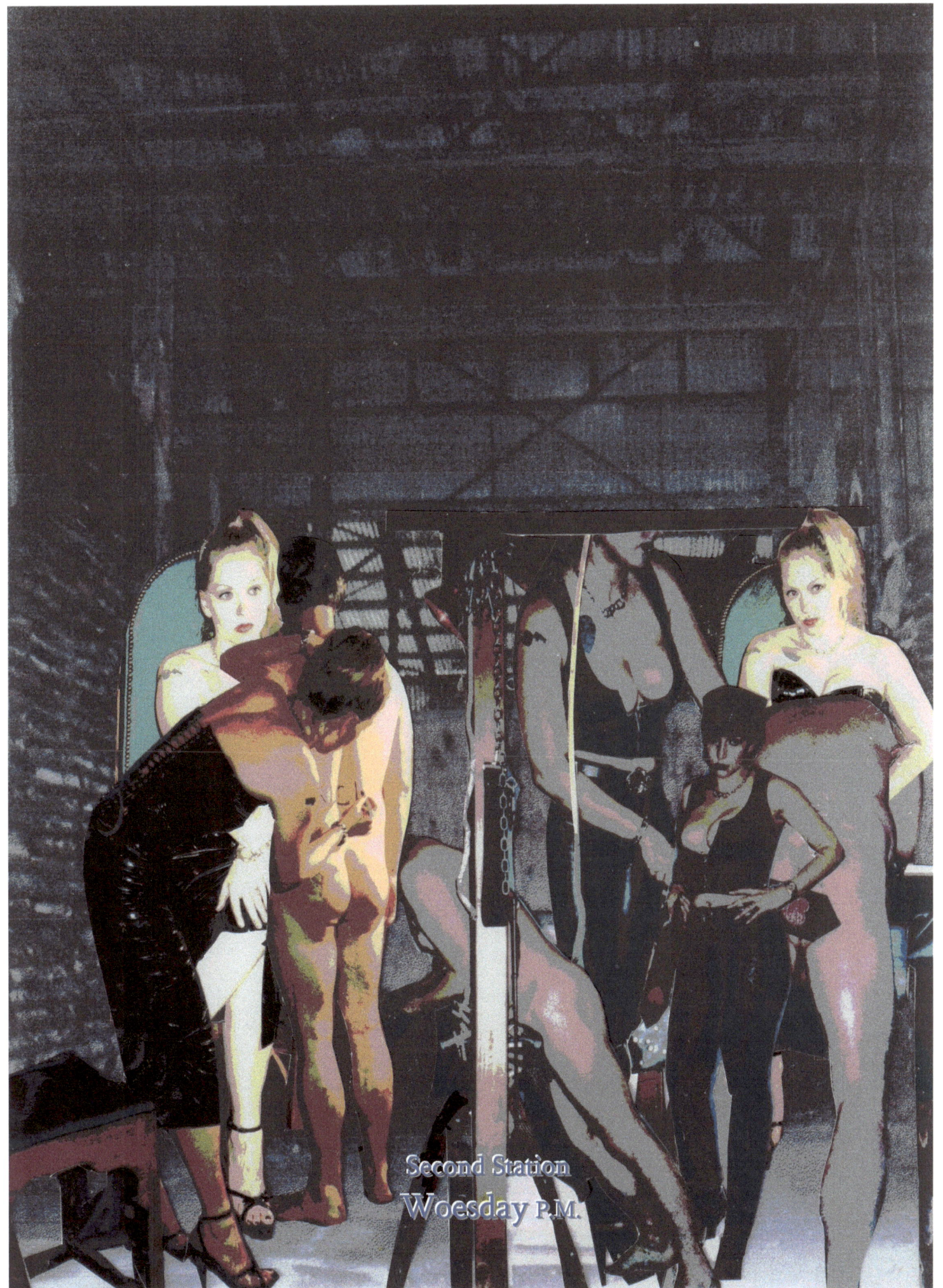

Second Station
Woesday P.M.

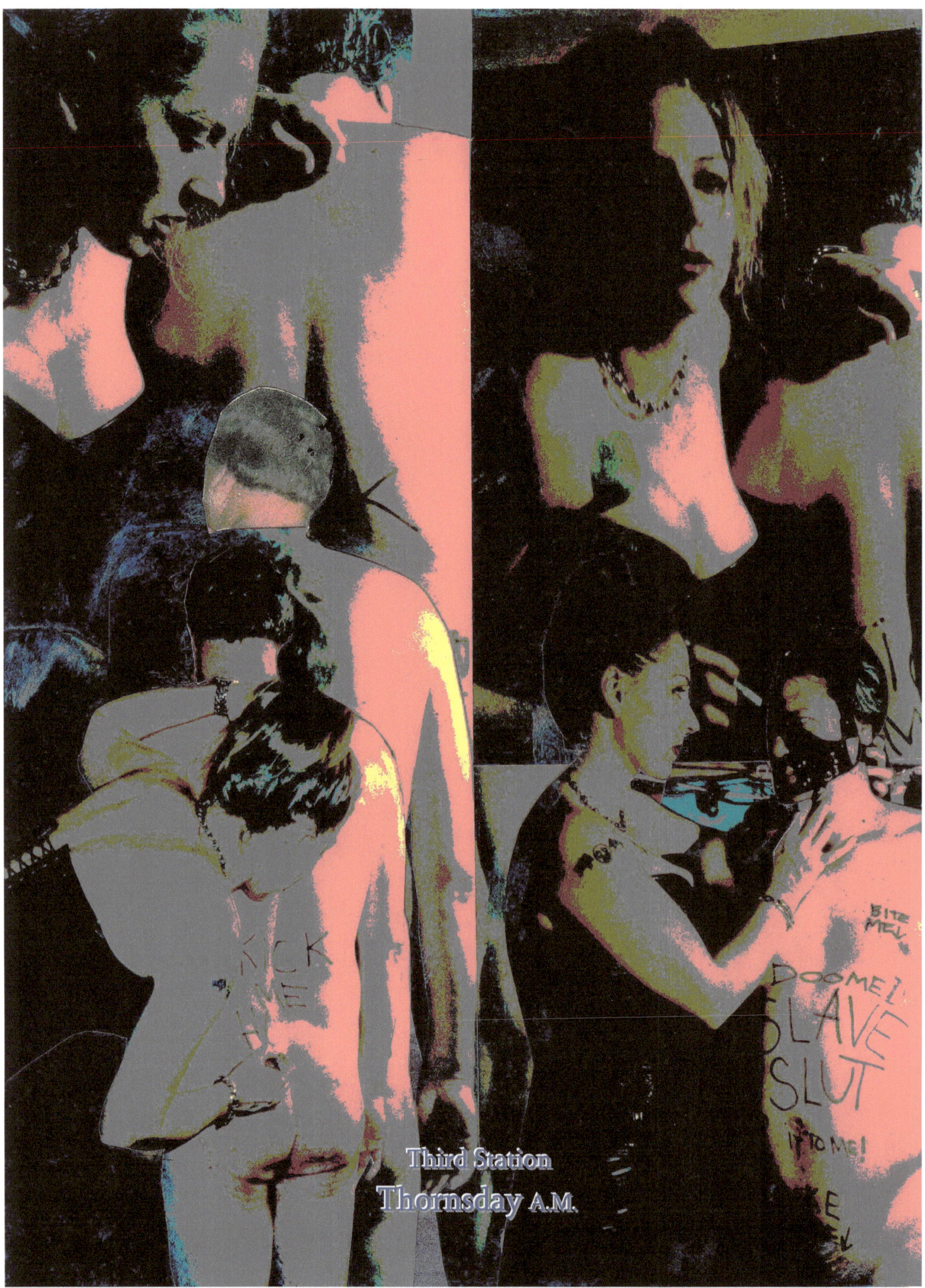

Third Station

Thornsday A.M.

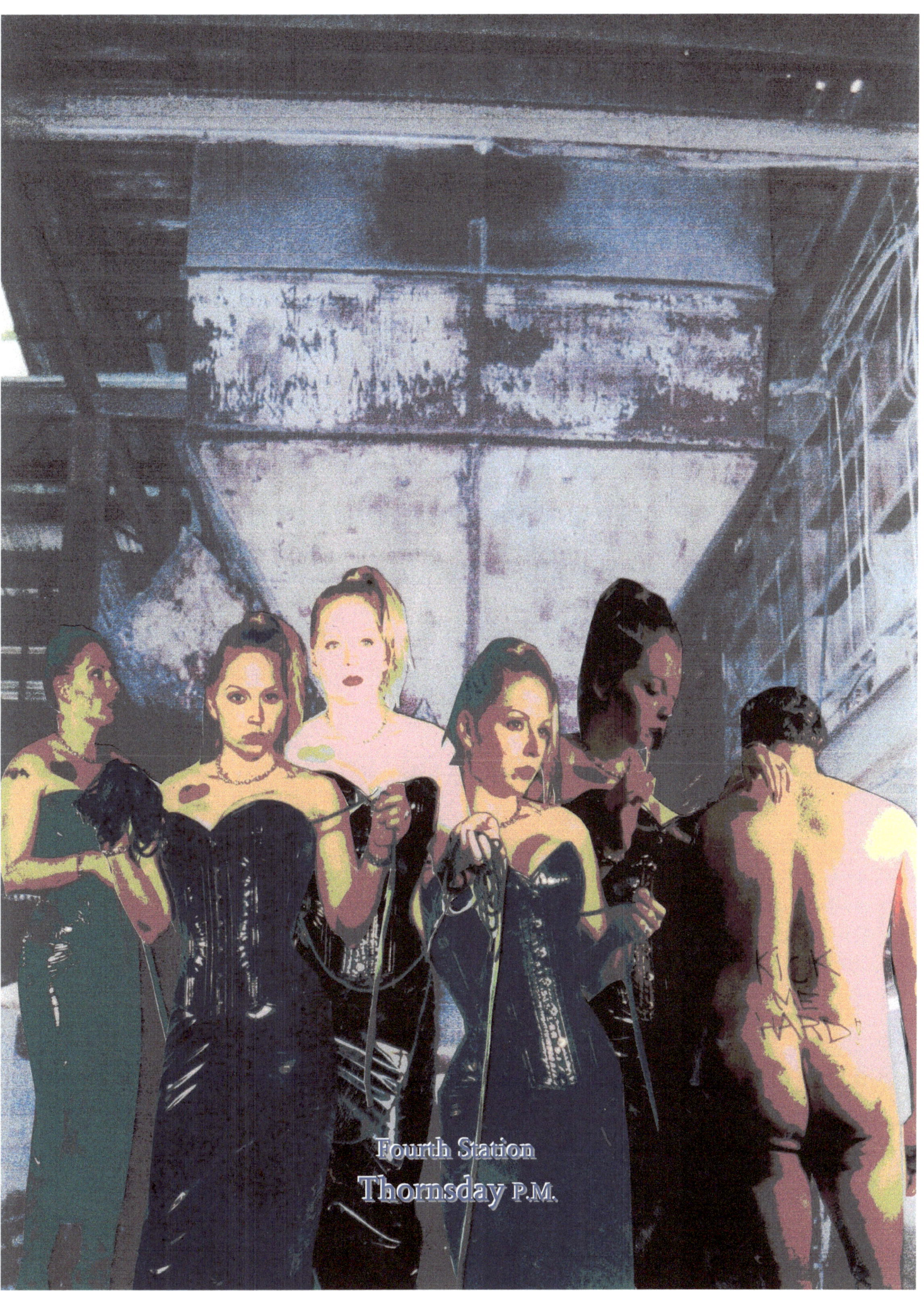

Fourth Station
Thornsday P.M.

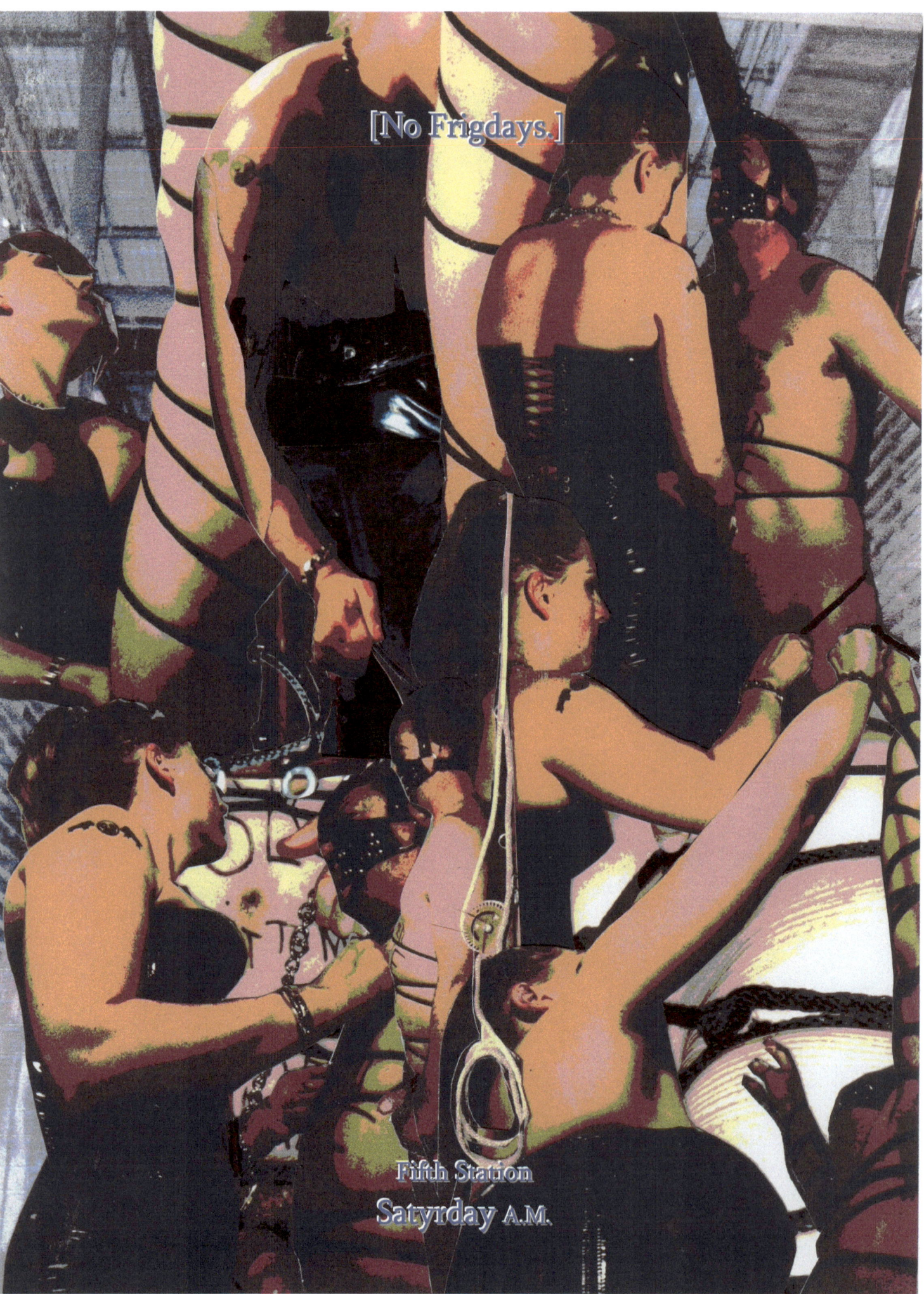

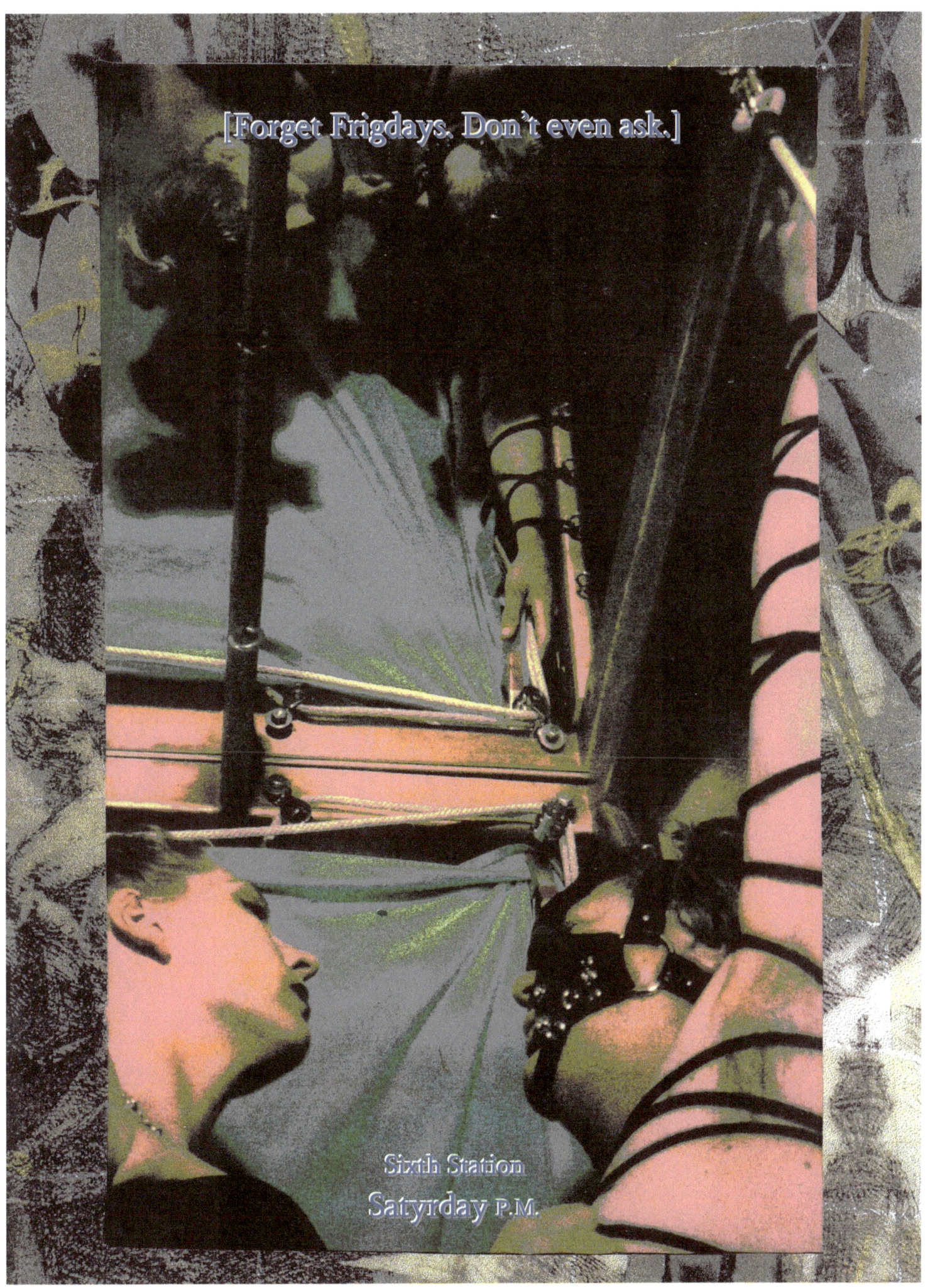

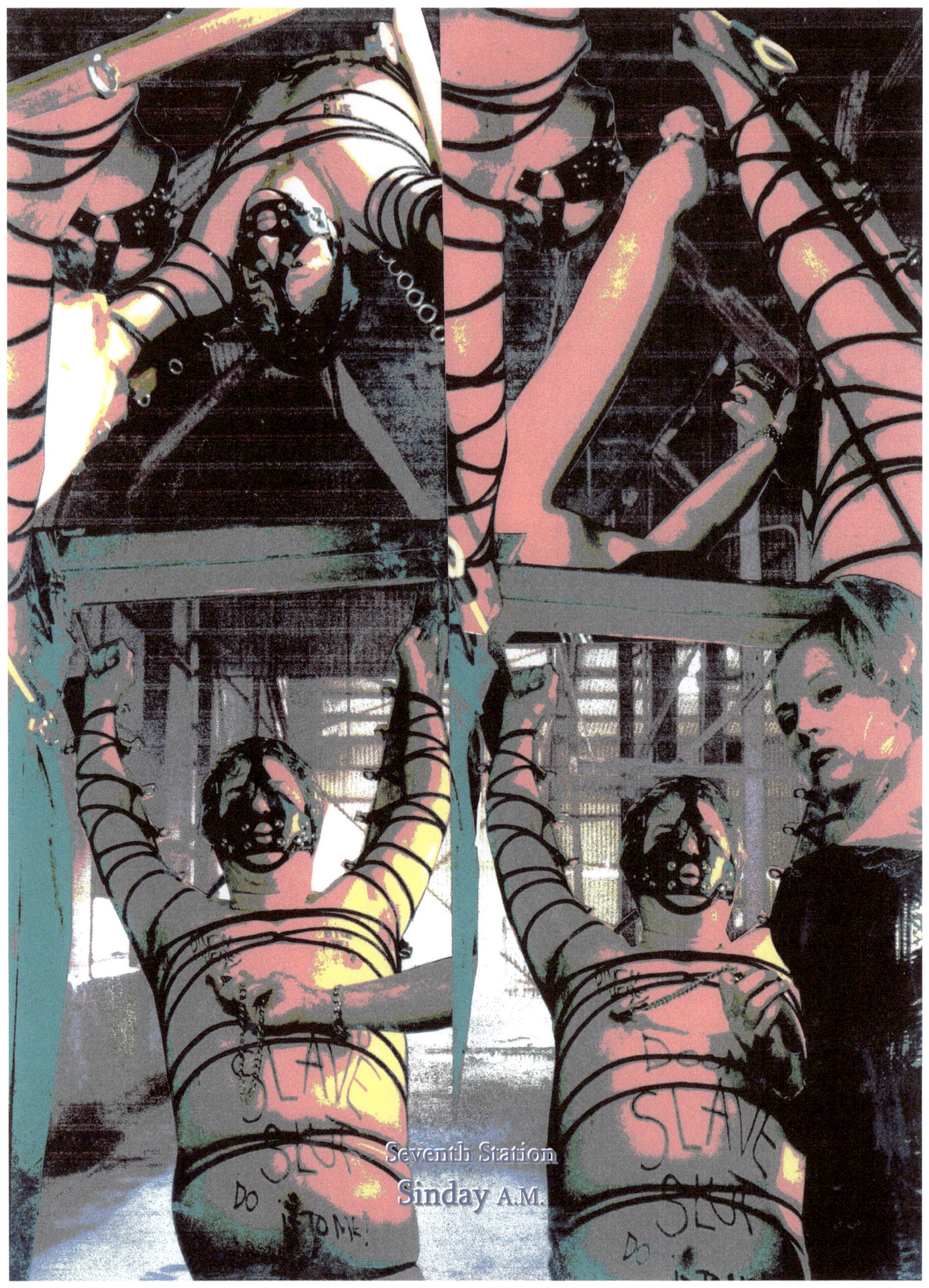

Seventh Station
Sinday A.M.

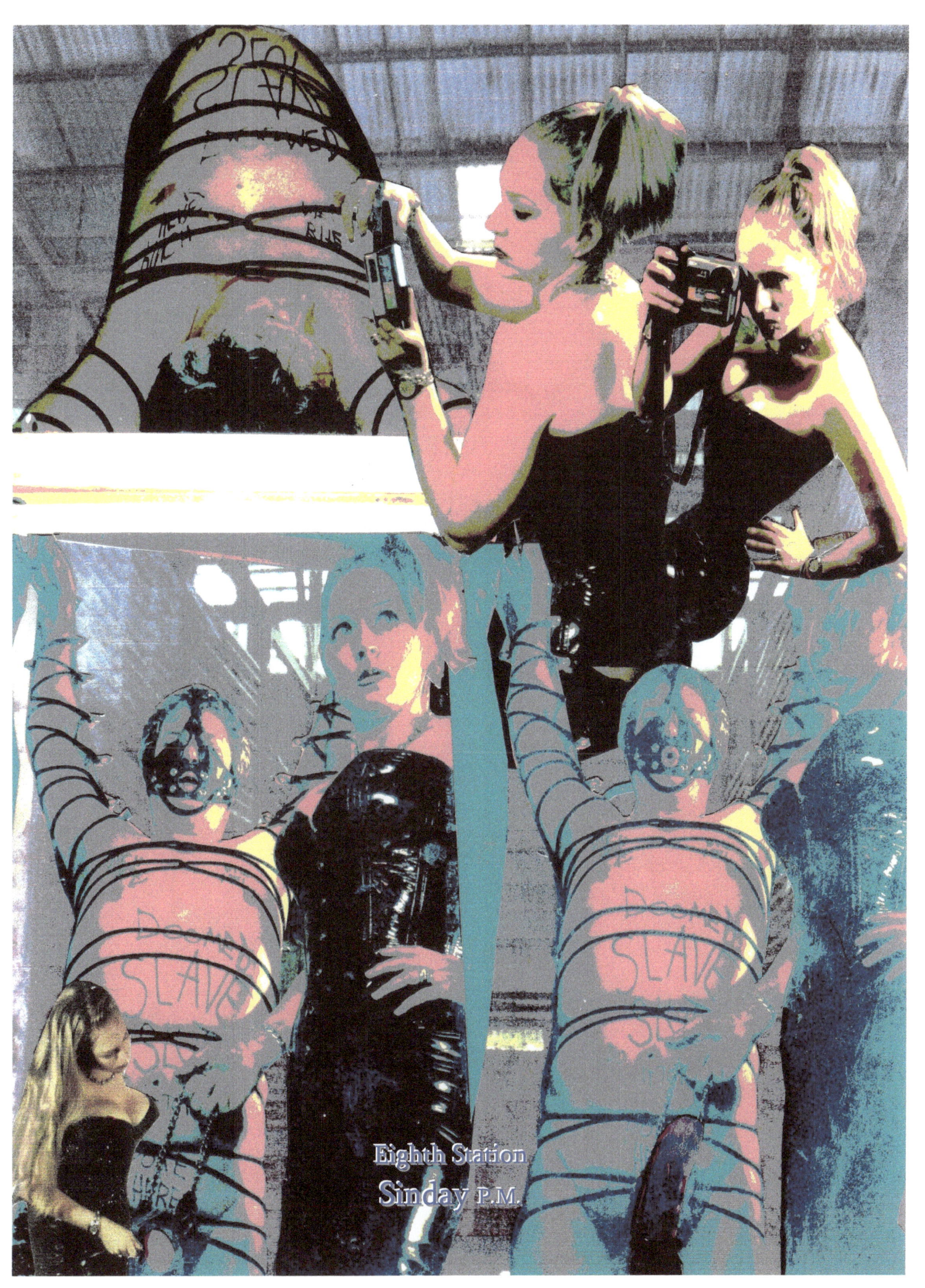

Eighth Station
Sinday P.M.

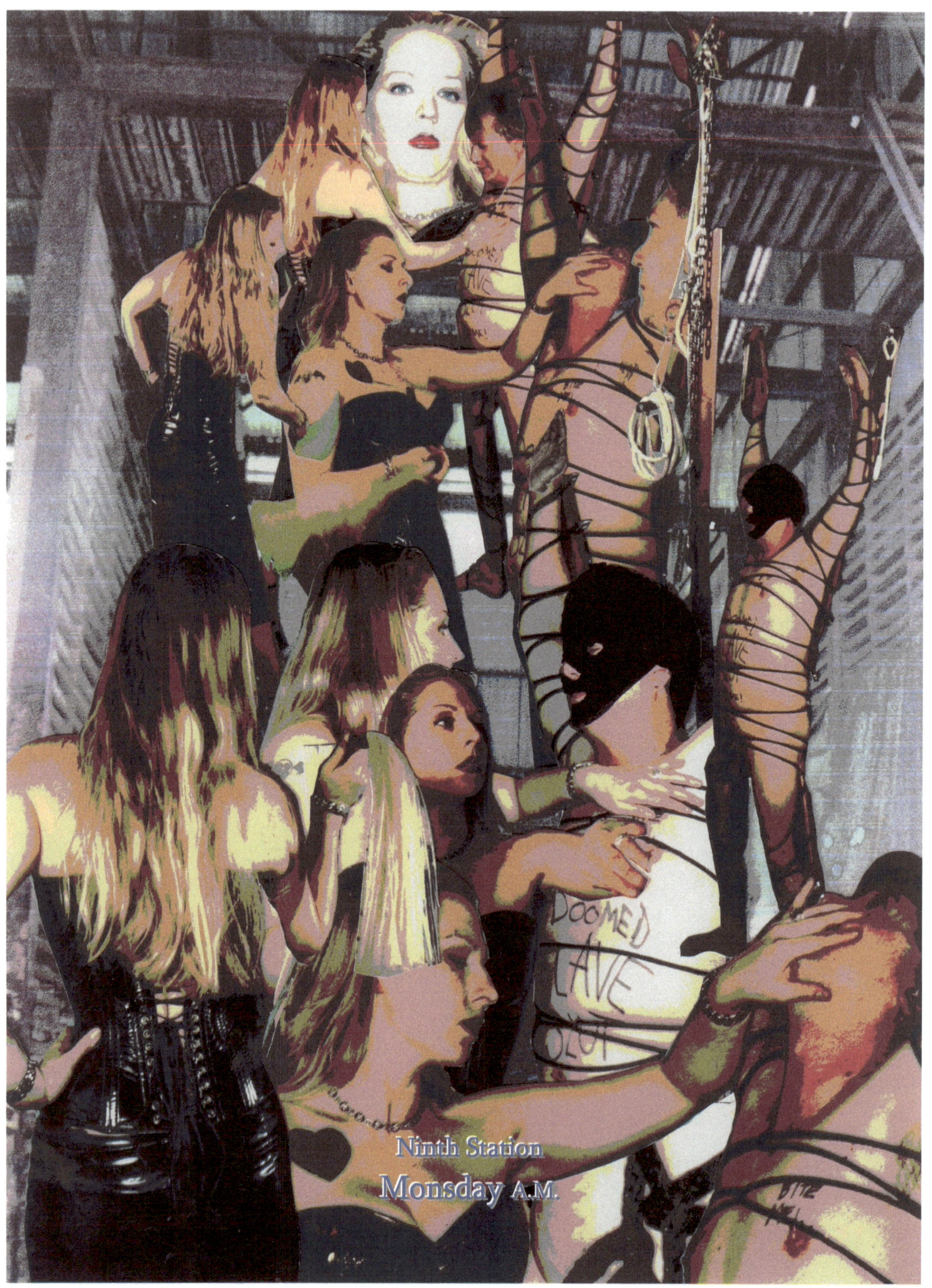

Ninth Station

Monsday A.M.

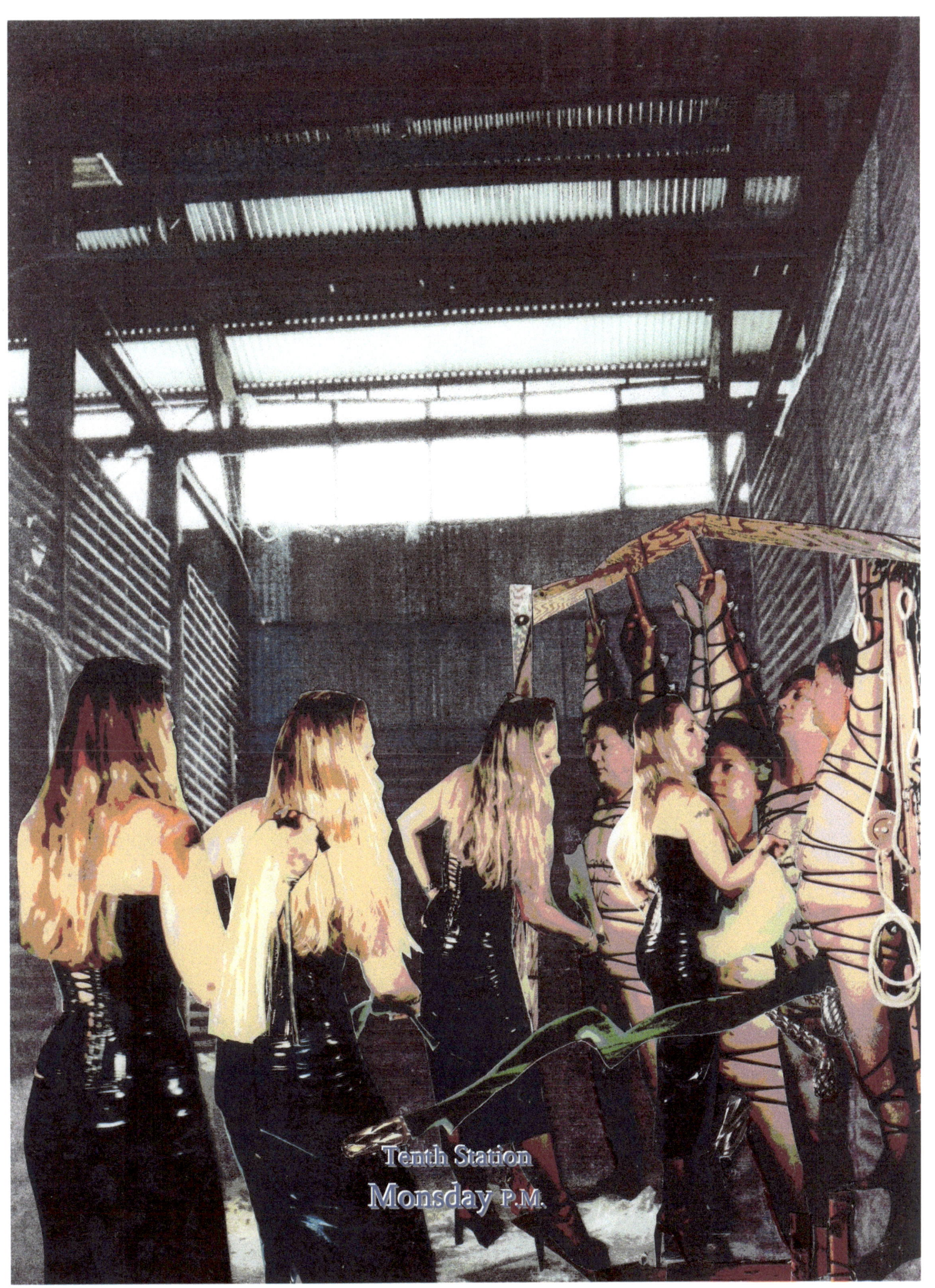

Tenth Station
Monsday P.M.

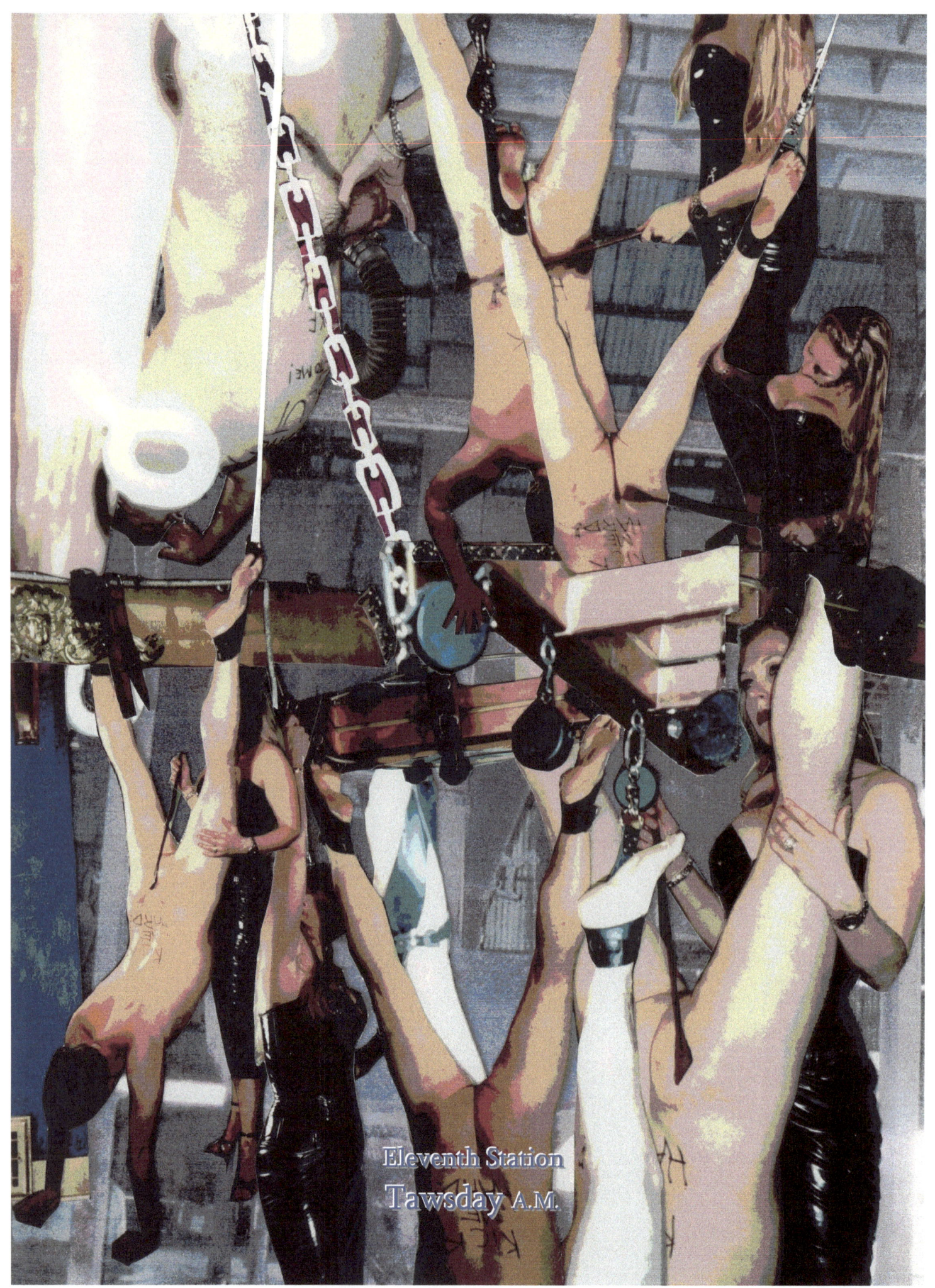

Eleventh Station
Tawsday A.M.

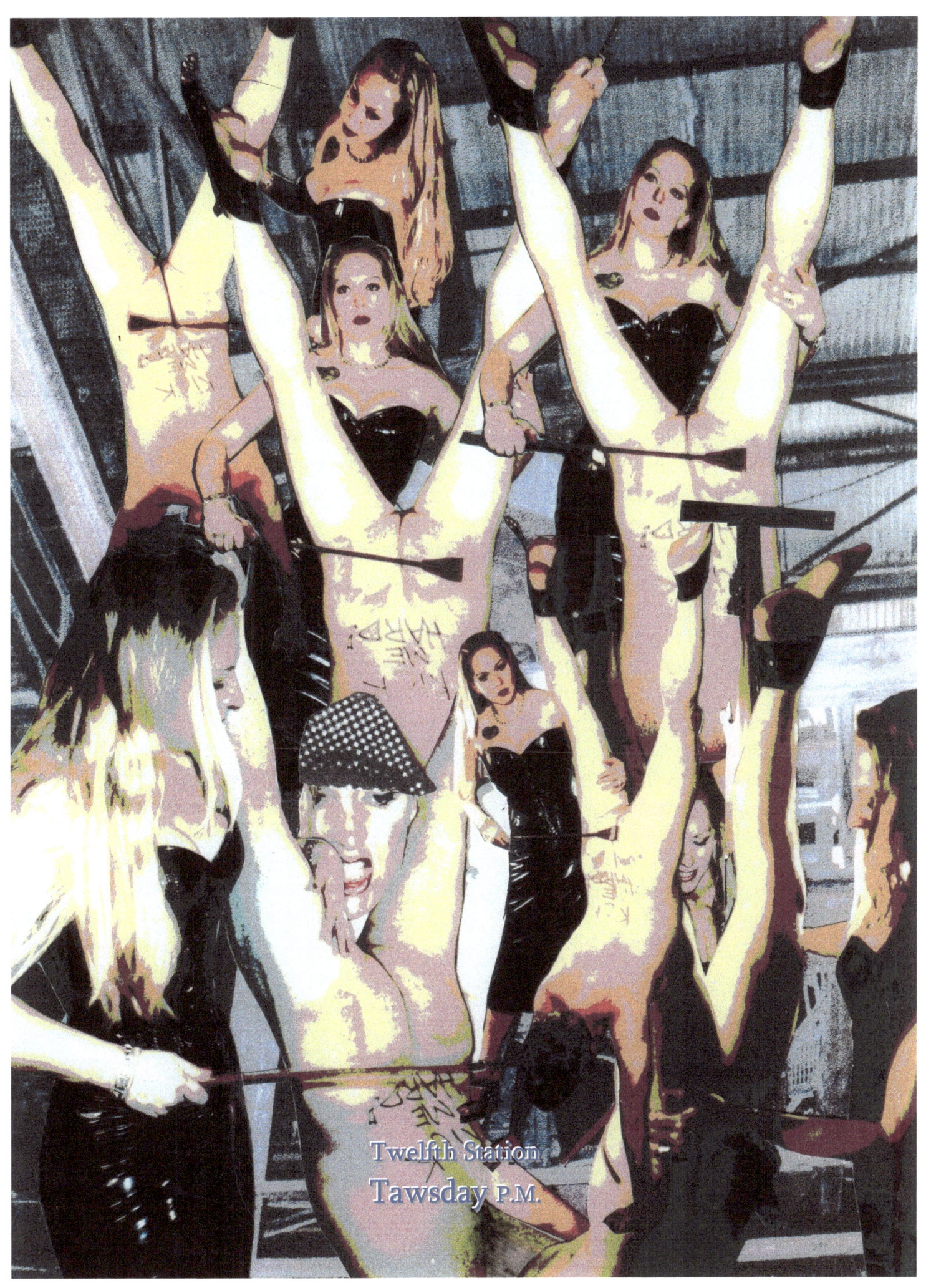

Twelfth Station
Tawsday P.M.

INTERMEZZO
Disciple Lashed

It seemed a lifetime ago that Lucrezia—"of The Cross"—peeked over her shoulder back down at me, staring up at her high rump romping like slap happy Ben Wa hams both vibrating off the other as they knocked about, slapping it up in my over amped libido while I followed her up the stairs from the street entrance where signage from the previous Garment District sweatshop still hung like an insider's joke. *Yes, no run of the mill **trim** here*, her piercing glance conveyed. On the landing, Lulu went to the first of a grand hallway full of oaken doors. "The Mistress will be with you presently," she swung open the massive door to the antechamber, "Please, take a seat."

In a blue lamp lit corner a coffin come wooden maiden leaned upright with cabinet door openings at face and crotch levels. With dabs of testosterone cream behind both ear lobes, I rejoined, "May I 'take' *yours?*"

Lucrezia held her poker face for three heartbeats before toying with a smile, "***Someone*** will have *somebody's* before the day is done, I'll wager," now grinning, she watched for her retort to impress my expression. My right eye cocked, "Now be a good boy and put your butt in that chair," she pointed to a metal studded contraption with immobilizing straps, "and save your enthusiasm for your coming ordeal with destiny." *Coming ordeal come coffin.*

The reverie demisted itself as I sat naked on my heels on the stone floor in the middle of the darkened chamber, gathering my wits after christening for twelve hours *each* the Twelve Stations of Sorrow. "Before being reborn," Mistress instructed from her throne, "one must first die." Illustra grinned as this initiate's shoulders tensed. *So predictable*, she surely mused. "Even if only metaphorically," she assuaged me, her latest tyro.

A slight drop in my shoulders told her, *Ahh, he's mine again.* "Before **change**, first there's **crisis**. We *here*, also, use stressors to create metamorphosis. Now off, catch us the foxes, for our vineyards are in bloom!"

Back out on the street after a gross of hours, the usual downtown tarryhoot was mute. Forsaken cars littered between emptied glassteelstone monoliths. Tumbleweednewsprint: "The Brutish are coming! The Brutish are coming!" Gothschild and Gilderberg, as per His Royal Highness's last request, had **Prince Philip** reincarnated as a killer virus taken up by the four winds.

Chapter 7
EXITUS
Diptych

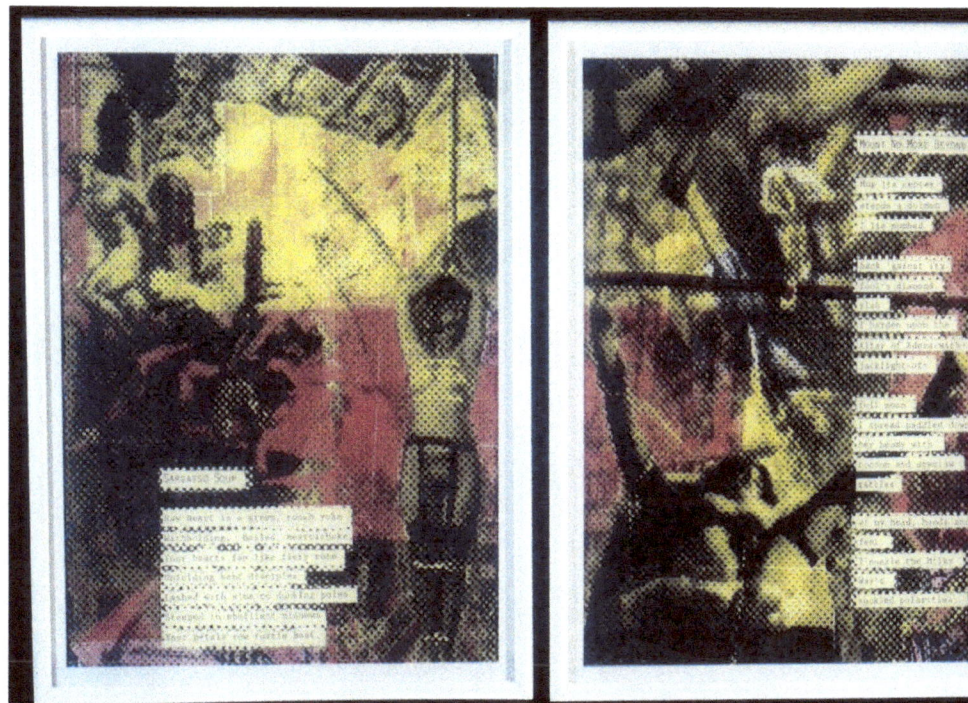

"Ask *not* what The State can do for you; ask what *you* can do for The State."—fr. *The Man Said 'Slide' So We Slid: confessions of a lamb lead to slaughter*

To: *Mistress Illustrious,*

Row me over the falls where primal screams trail off into electro mist dreams roaring into a rapturous body aripple with your romping buoyancy. Without you I am a murky pool. Stagnate. A mud puddle. A smudge on the worn sole of a discarded shoe...

'till abuzz within the sweet, swarming sting of your honeycombed promise. 'Till then I await your pleasure in hive-honored dance signing the sky with your pollen-potent name, my Royal Jellied Highness.

'Till then, I am

Your bumbling drone,

Fr: *Smikes!*

SARGASSO SOUP

Raw heart is a green, tough yoke
Withholding. Boiled, Heartichoke,
Your bracts fan like fiery rose
Unfolding kept disciples
Lashed with vine to dunking poles
Steeped in ebullient minnows
Your petals row turtle boat.

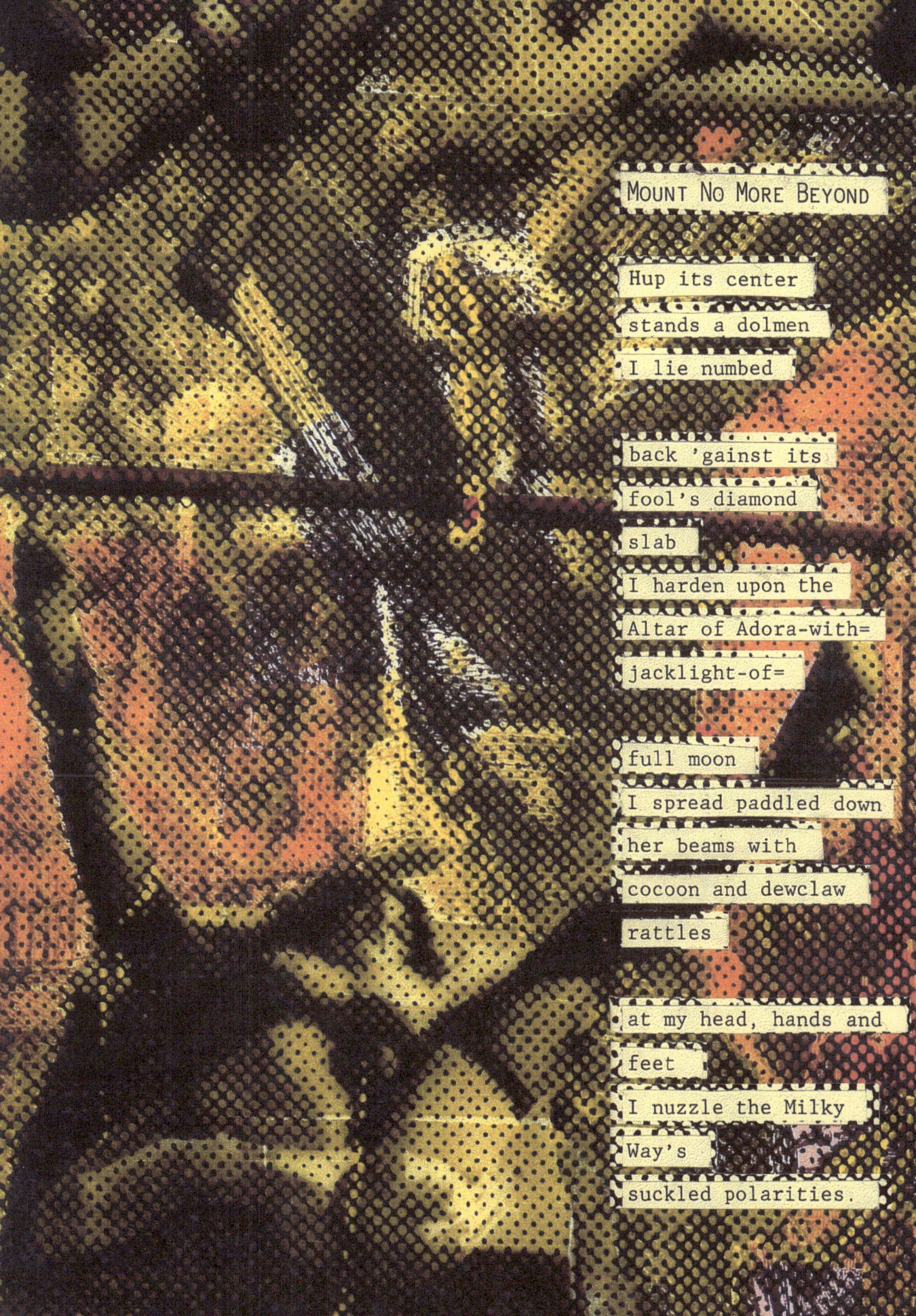

MOUNT NO MORE BEYOND

Hup its center
stands a dolmen
I lie numbed

back 'gainst its
fool's diamond
slab
I harden upon the
Altar of Adora-with=
jacklight-of=

full moon
I spread paddled down
her beams with
cocoon and dewclaw
rattles

at my head, hands and
feet
I nuzzle the Milky
Way's
suckled polarities.

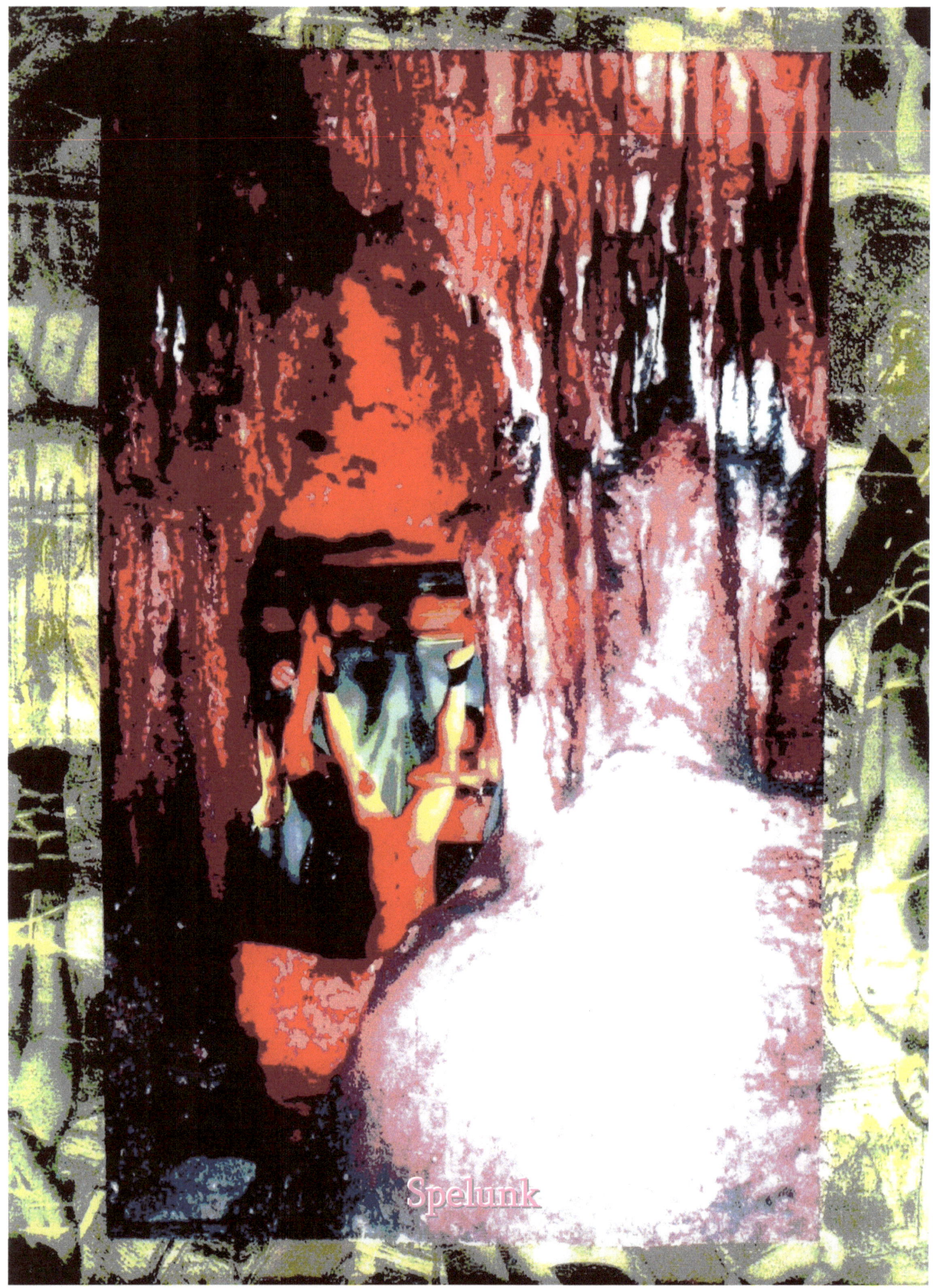
Spelunk

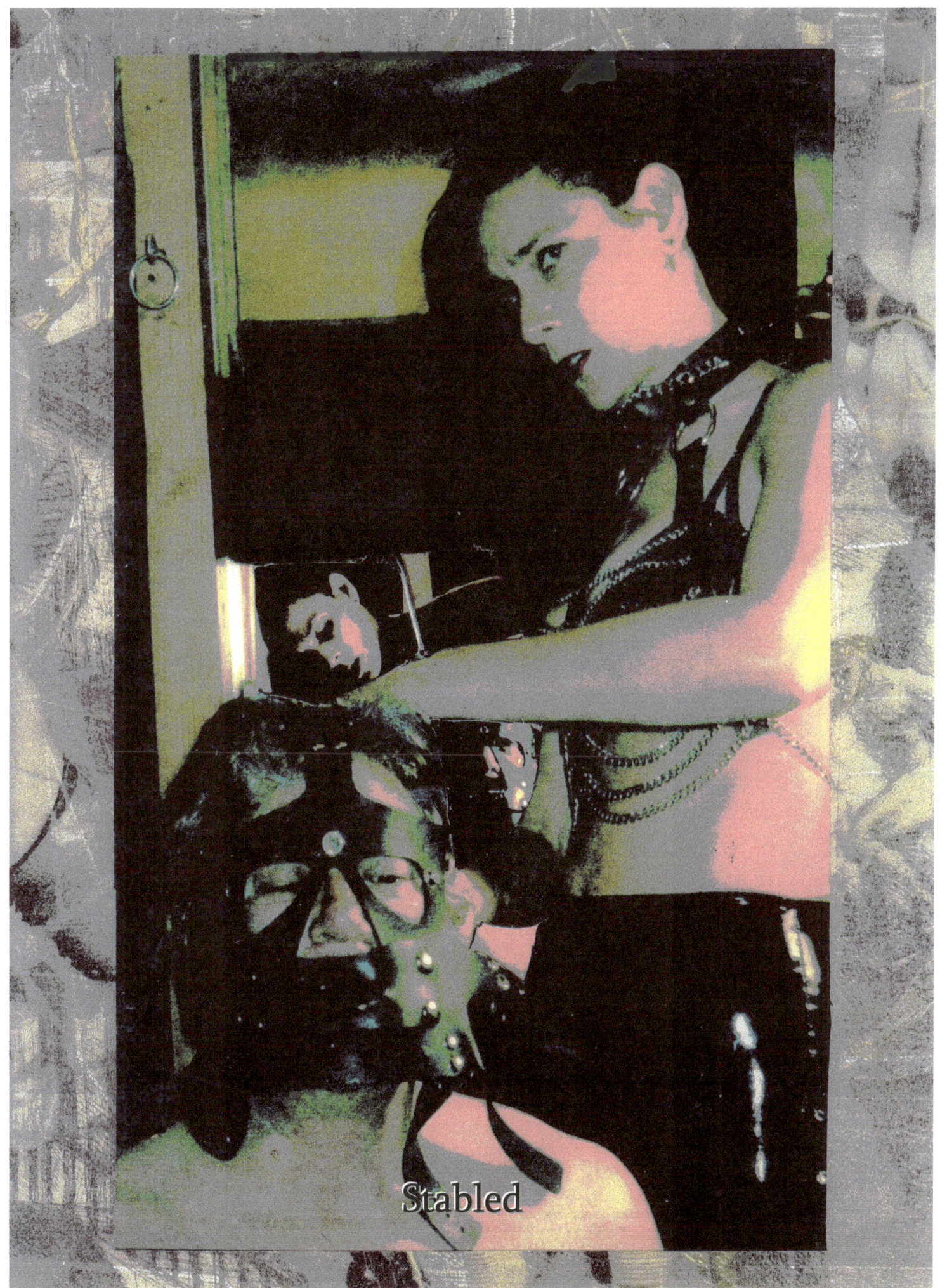

Stabled

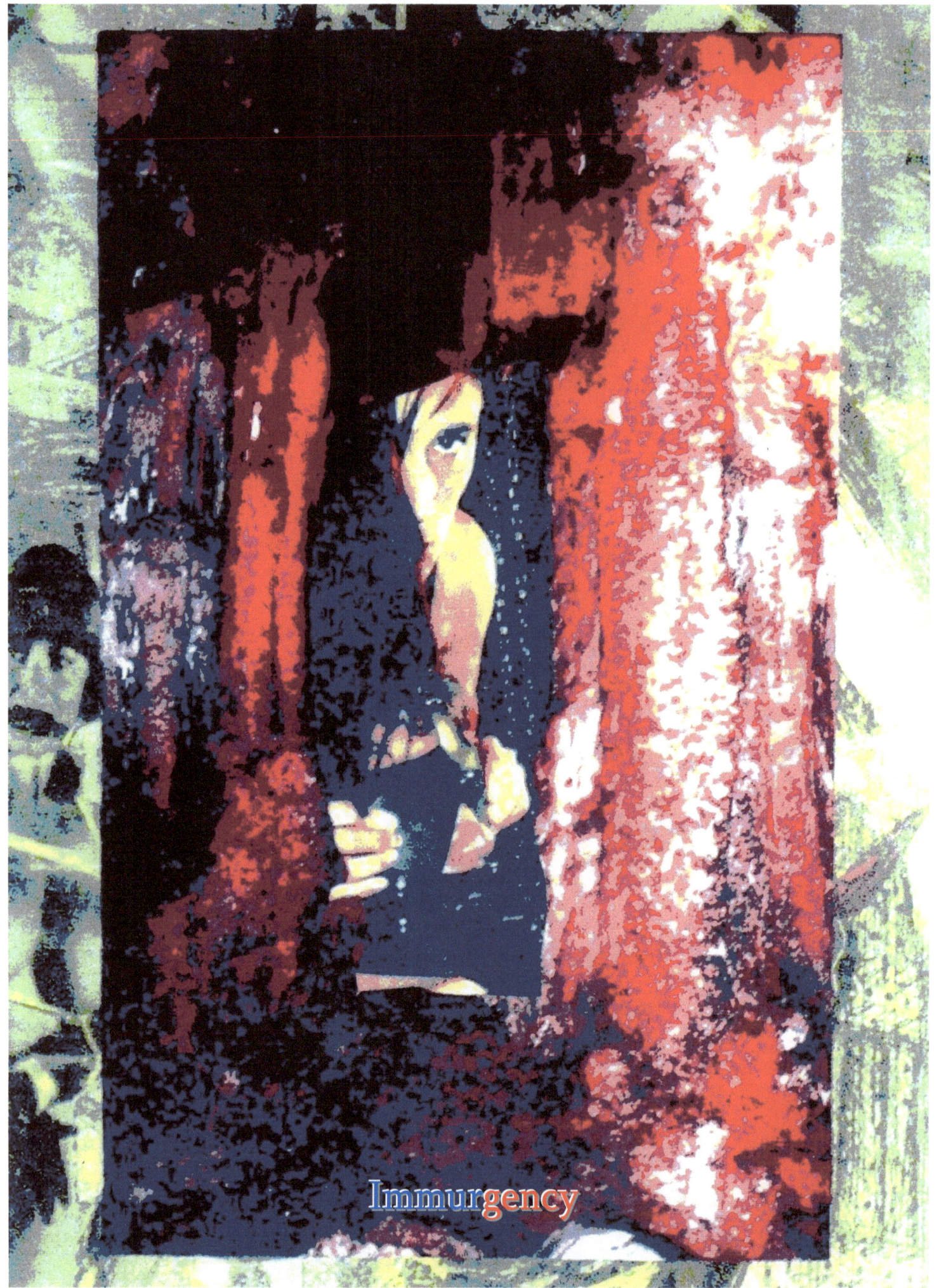

Immurgency

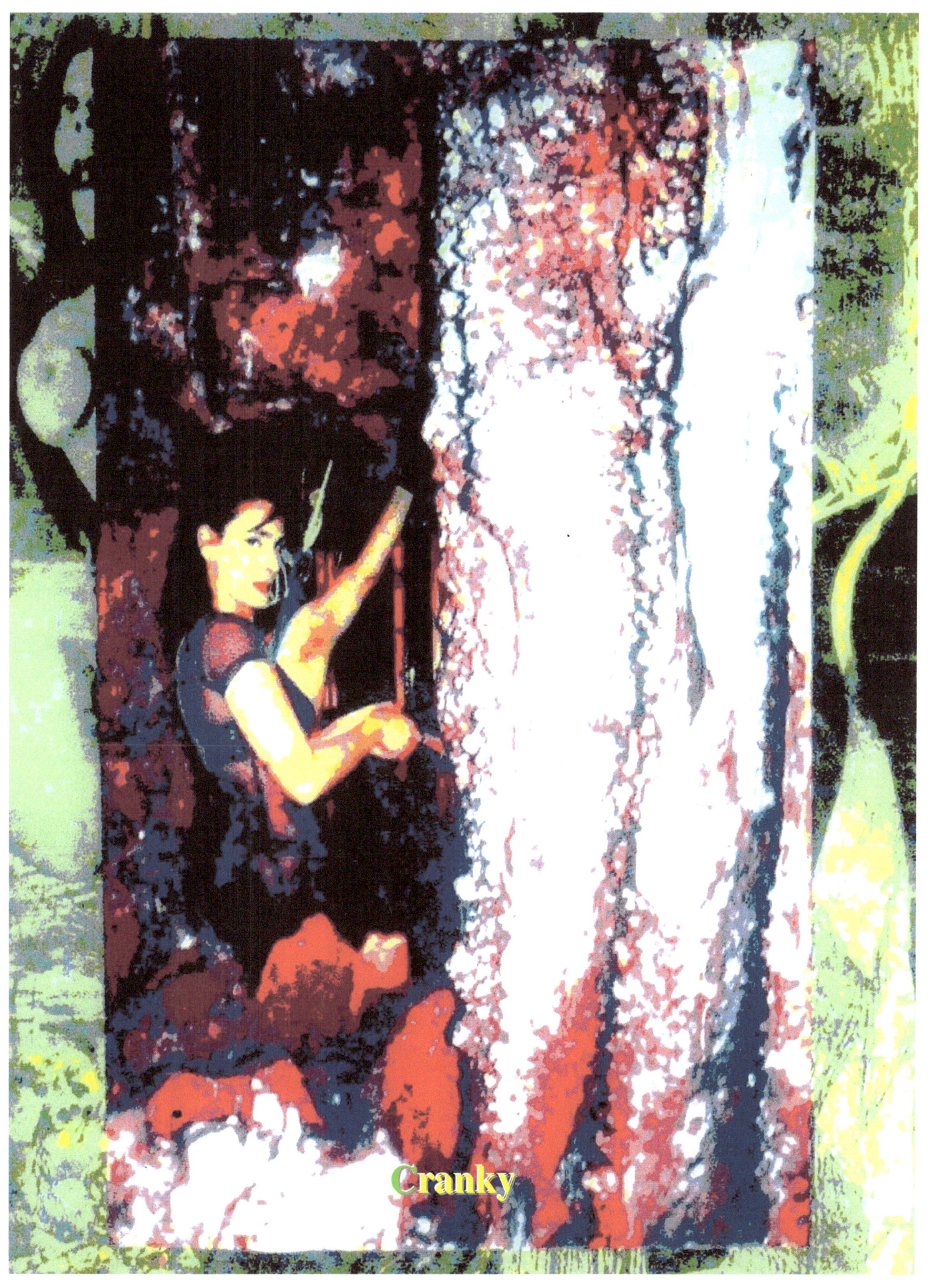

Cranky

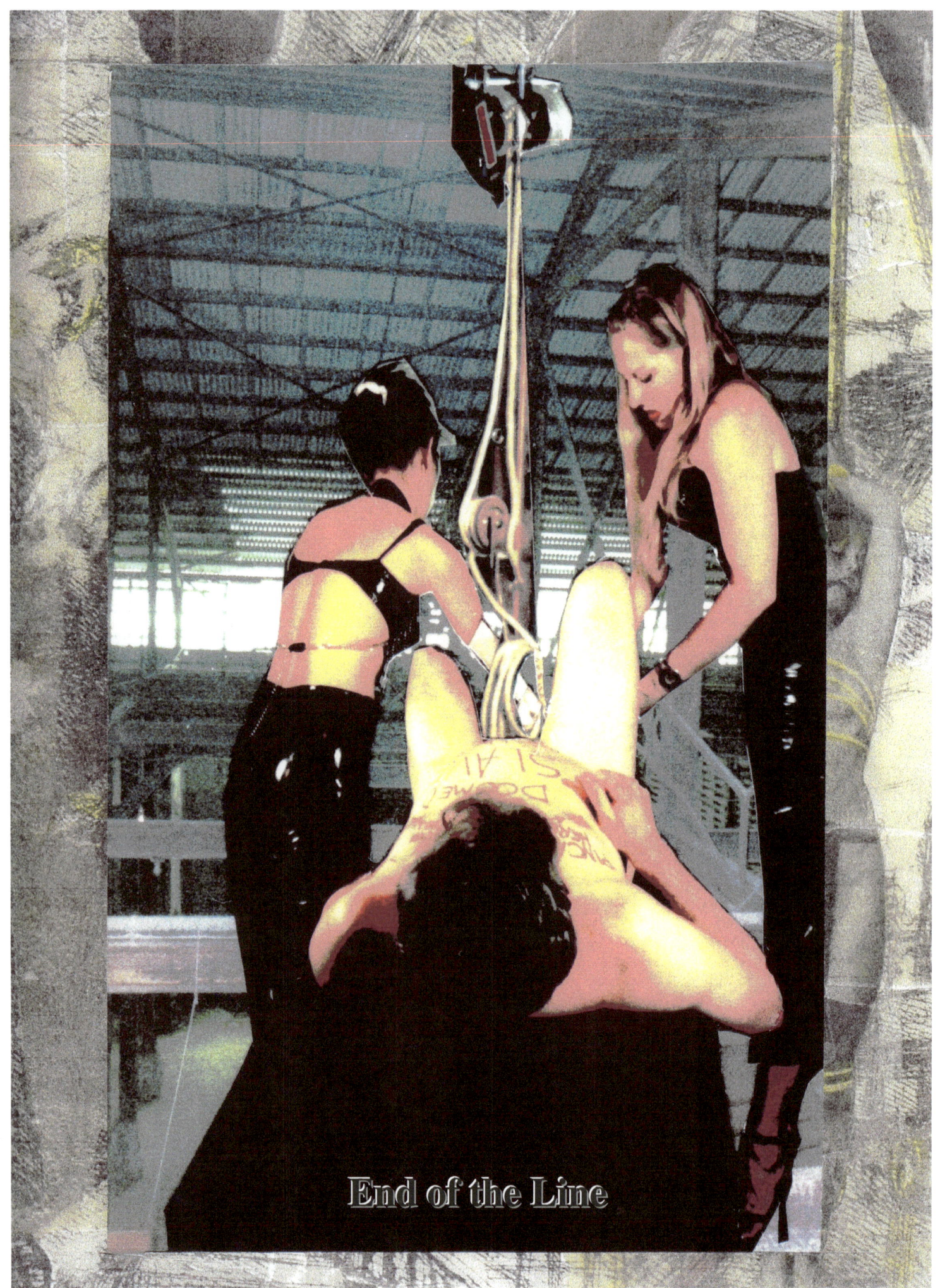

End of the Line

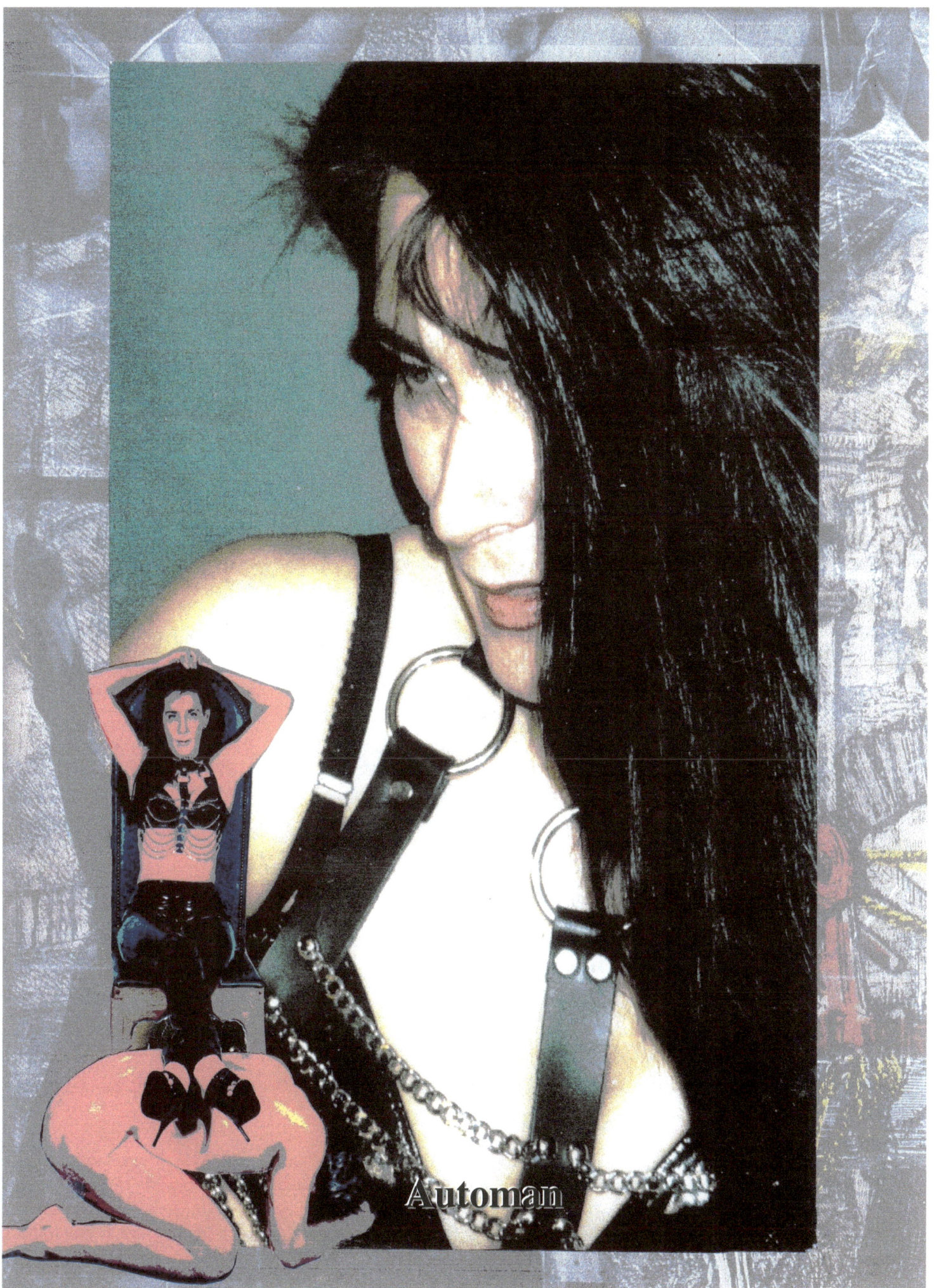

Automan

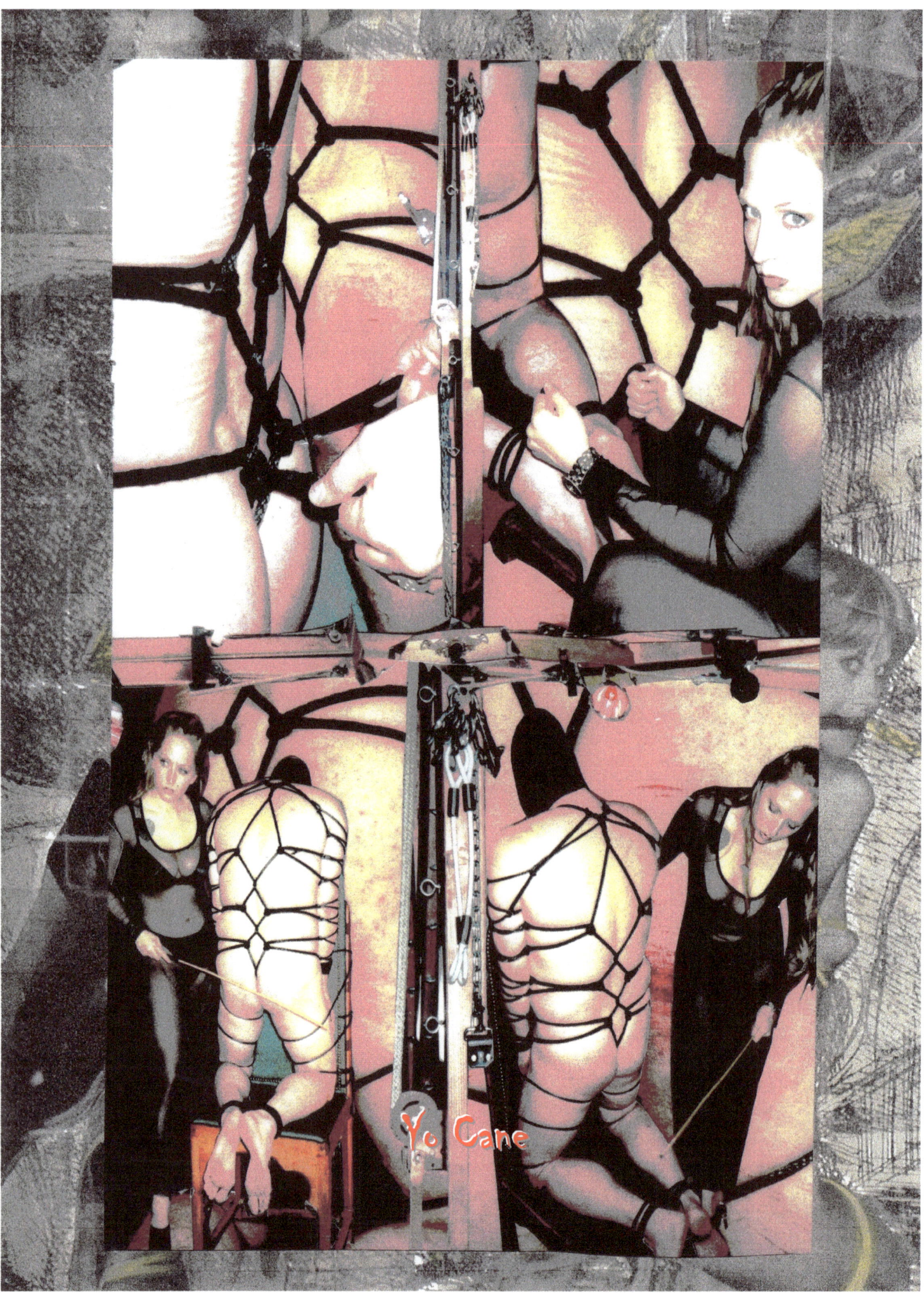

Chapter 8
MOONSTOCKS
Diptych

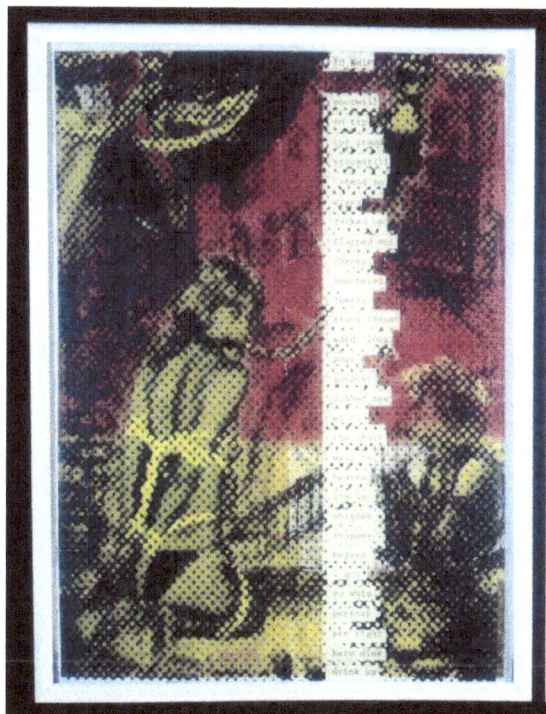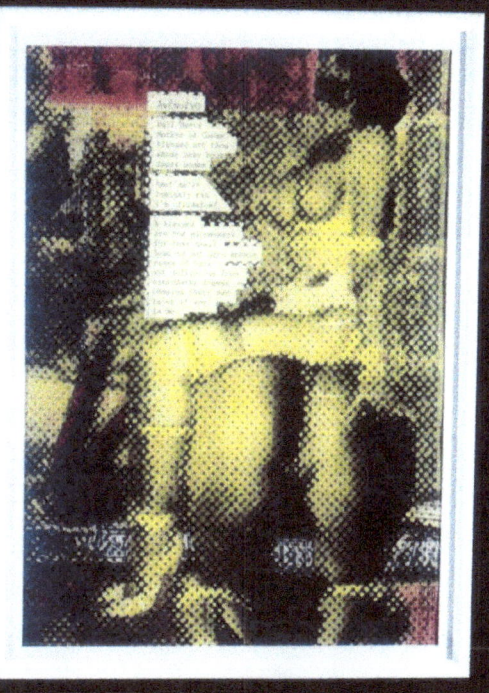

"Semi-precious" *Nun Jade* loved making men squirm under heel. Loved to escort each naked on a leash to Sanctum von Kix. *Await their asses whipped.*

posted: *I am* **Velum,** *Words on the Cross,* Worte am Kreuz; *I am* **knot**chen, *tangled lumps,* Mein Gottin, ***My Goddess*** von Kummer Zitzen, ***of Suffering Titties!*** *I am your altar,* *my* **Pitmos**trocity, *through me rise from Hell this spring we'll retrace* wie die linien **wacklen,** *how the lines* **wobble** *whackin' out* new chevrons flayed over old,
fulfilling not destroying,
signed: ***Lance*** **von** ***Longinus.*** date:**33-0430 Novus Ordo Mundi.**witness:***Punishe Pilates.***

We ferment in the Bowel of the Beast. A bevy bunkered. All bent over frottage bobposts, every navel a tight cluster of **knots** each puckered over gut punch pressure switch on thoraxis drive juddering to dithereens *atandem.*

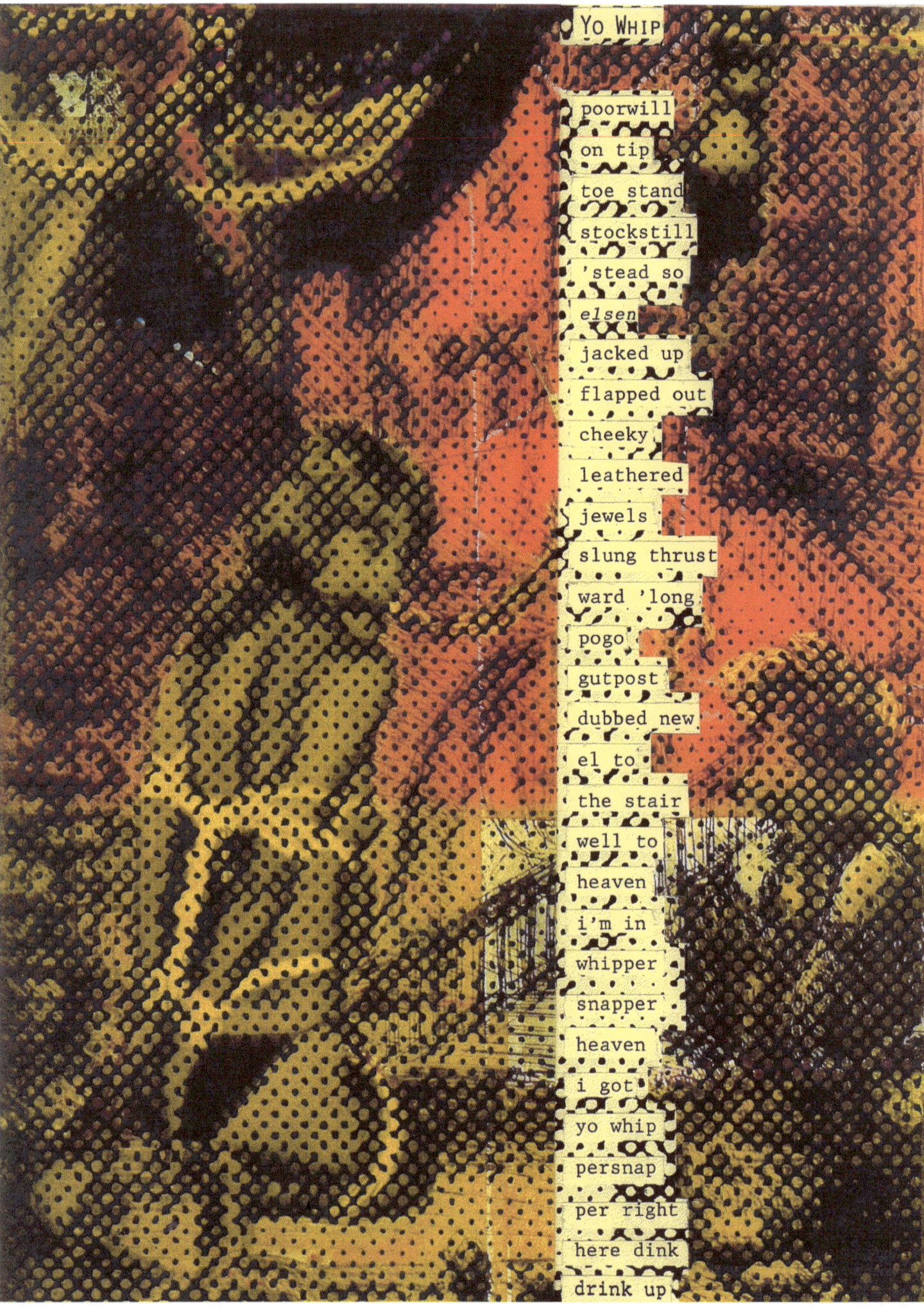

YO WHIP

poorwill
on tip
toe stand
stockstill
'stead so
elsen
jacked up
flapped out
cheeky
leathered
jewels
slung thrust
ward 'long
pogo
gutpost
dubbed new
el to
the stair
well to
heaven
i'm in
whipper
snapper
heaven
i got
yo whip
persnap
per right
here dink
drink up

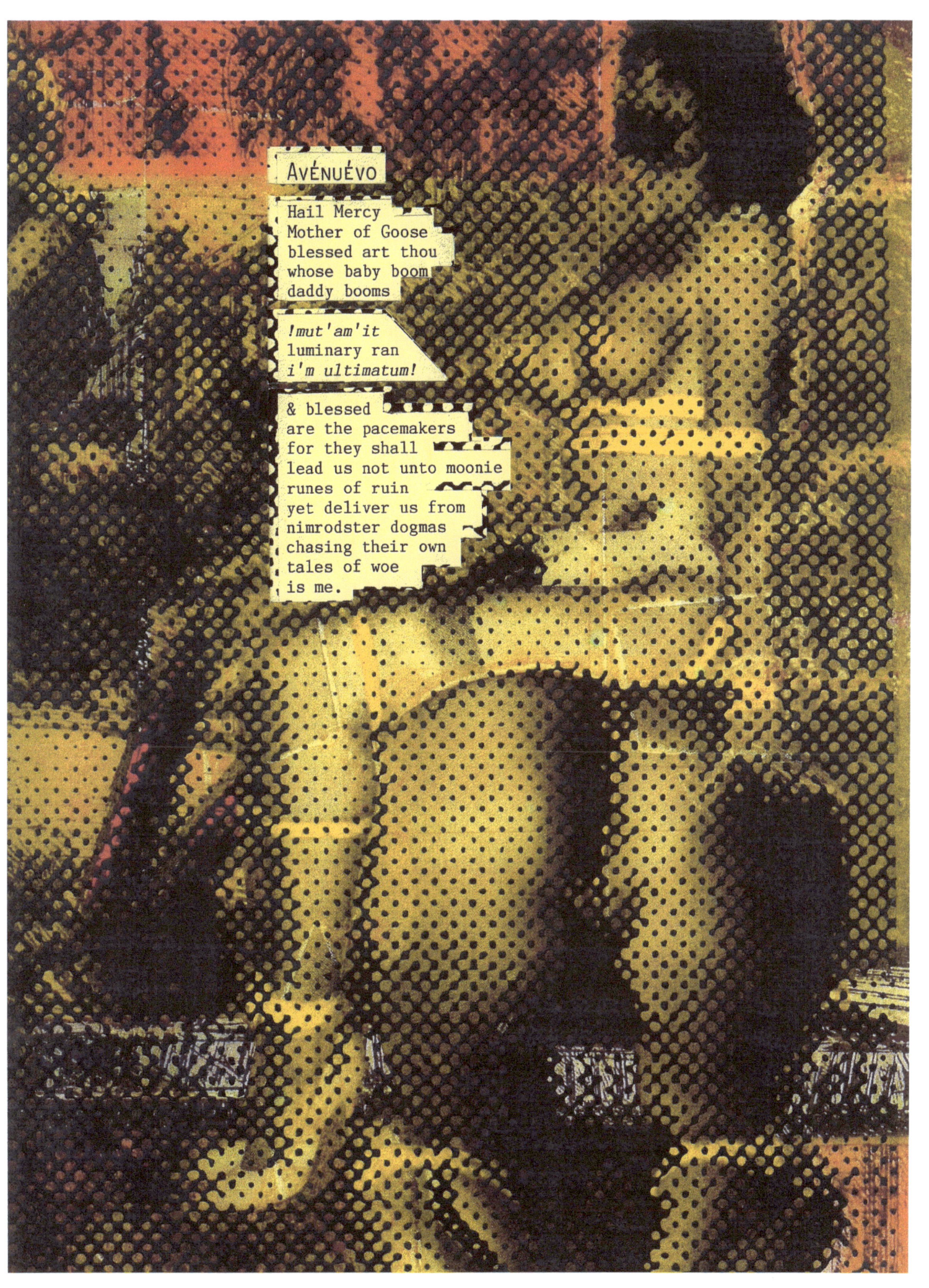

Avénuévo

Hail Mercy
Mother of Goose
blessed art thou
whose baby boom
daddy booms

!mut'am'it
luminary ran
i'm ultimatum!

& blessed
are the pacemakers
for they shall
lead us not unto moonie
runes of ruin
yet deliver us from
nimrodster dogmas
chasing their own
tales of woe
is me.

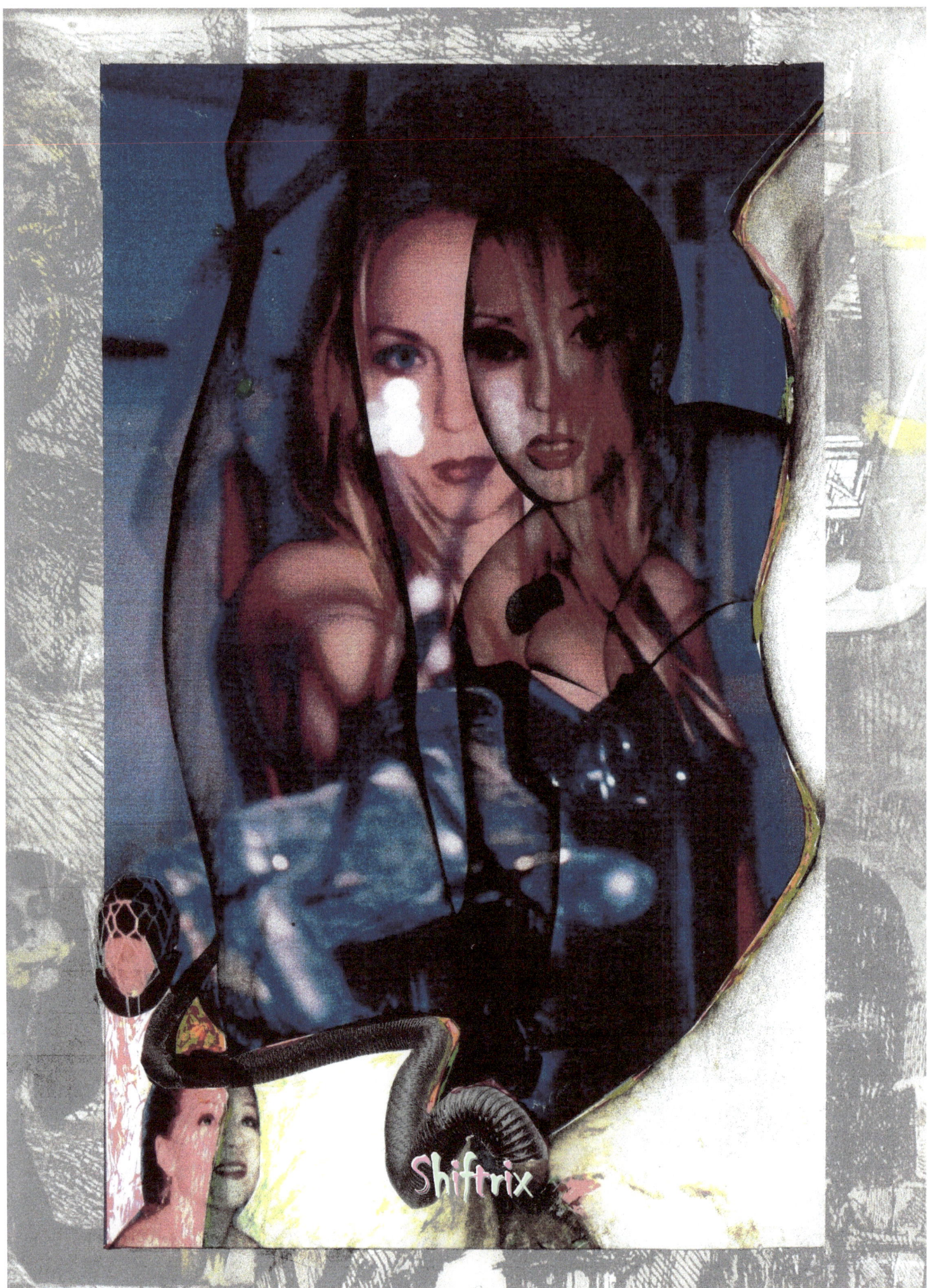

Shiftrix

Chapter 9
CRACKPOT
Diptych

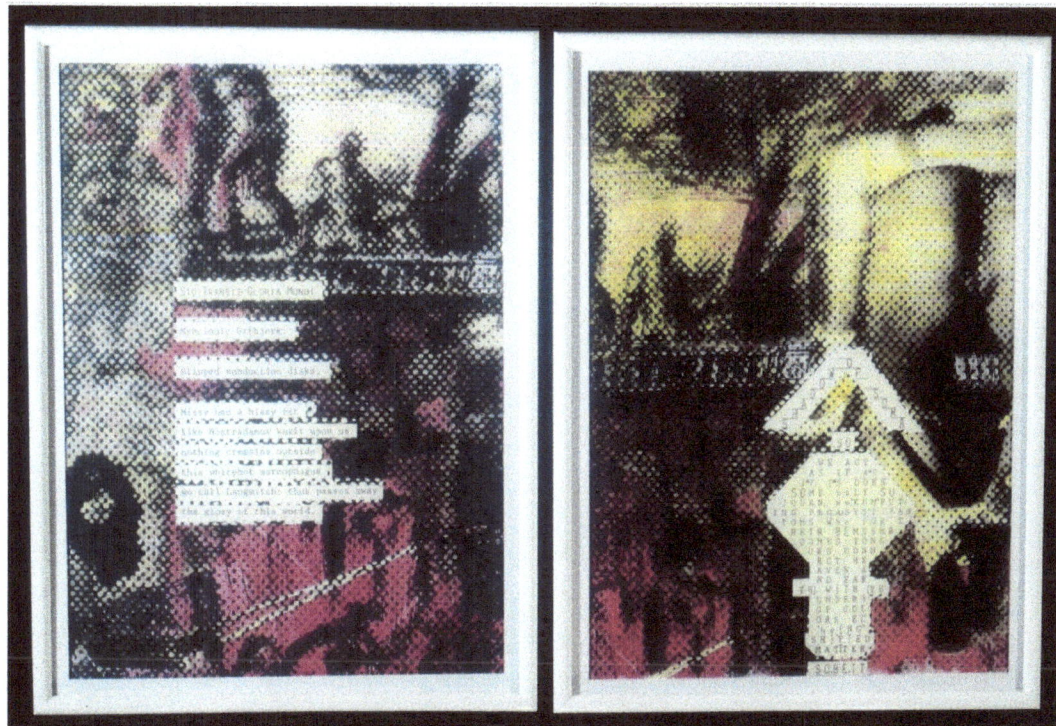

It takes the juice of a school of **useless breathers** hung out to dry for inking a *Versus Intexti*. Each **youbē** a hump engine piston chugging autogyrally, cursively, sewn together by our common thread: *Illustra,* whose design is to dry hump the con**trap**tion into a rapt seizure as metal shavings spit out smoky aluminum oxide streamers of a nano-crystalline mist culled to silver a chemtrailed perma-web univiewer sky **topside** looming forth The Hologrammaton scaring shit out of the *genpop* just so to get them queued in: *Left shoulders against the wall! Shirts tucked in! Hands in pockets! Stack it up, nuts to butts!* **Gawd** was restored to the sky. **Trixtress,** a kiss **below.**

The Final Crusade's a great diversion. General Sun Tsu say, "*All* war is deception." Armies of Armageddon were all plowshared far from homes with doors left wide open for the marauding horde called the **Cremators of Care.**

Revelations <u>9</u>:<u>11</u> *They had as king over them the angel of the **Abyss.***

SIC TRANSIT GLORIA MUNDI

Myoclonic Urthjerk.

Slipped subduction disks.

Missy had a hissy fit
like Nostradamus knelt upon us
nothing cremains outside
this whitehot sarcophagus
we call Langwitch: thus passes away
the glory of this world.

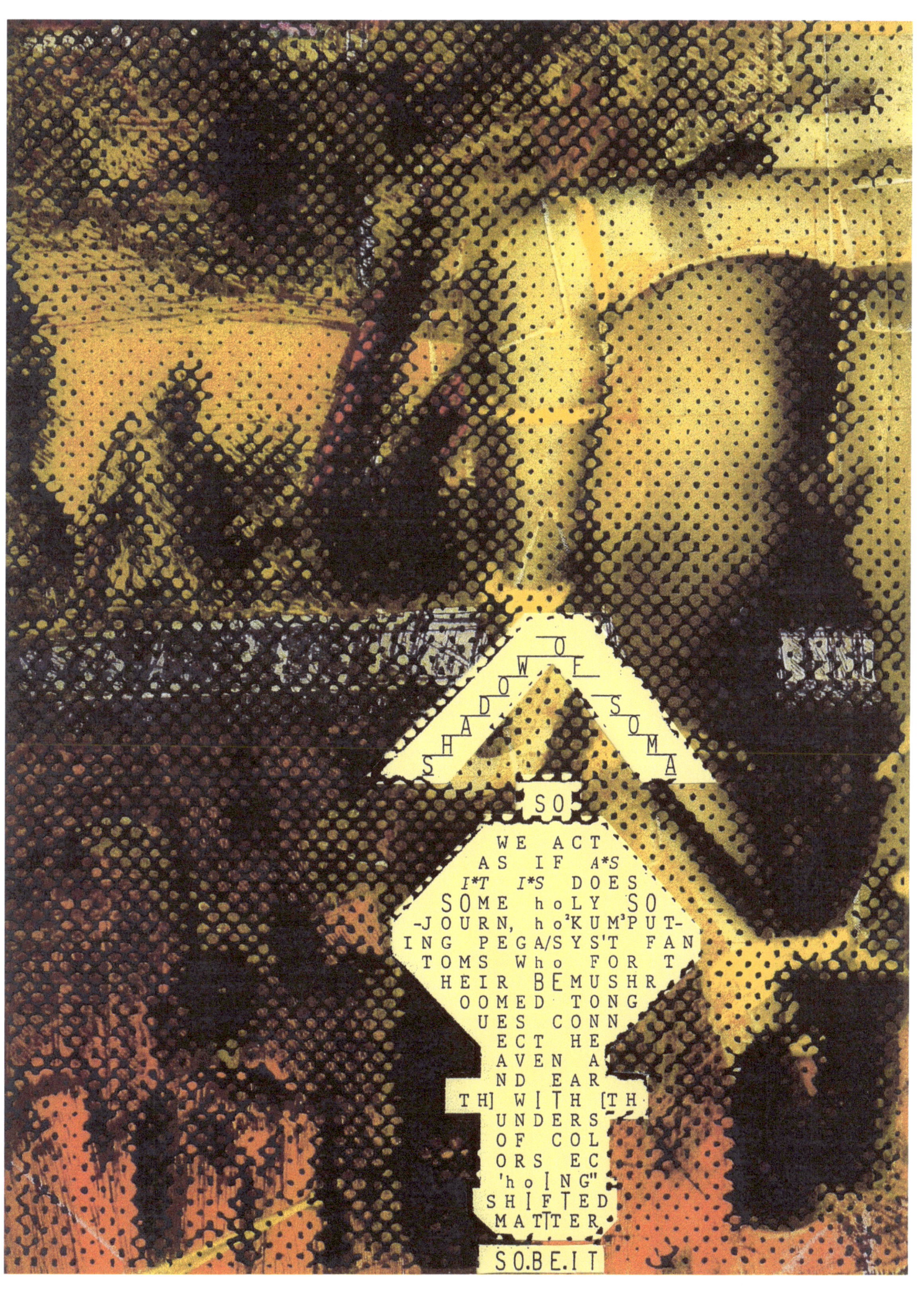

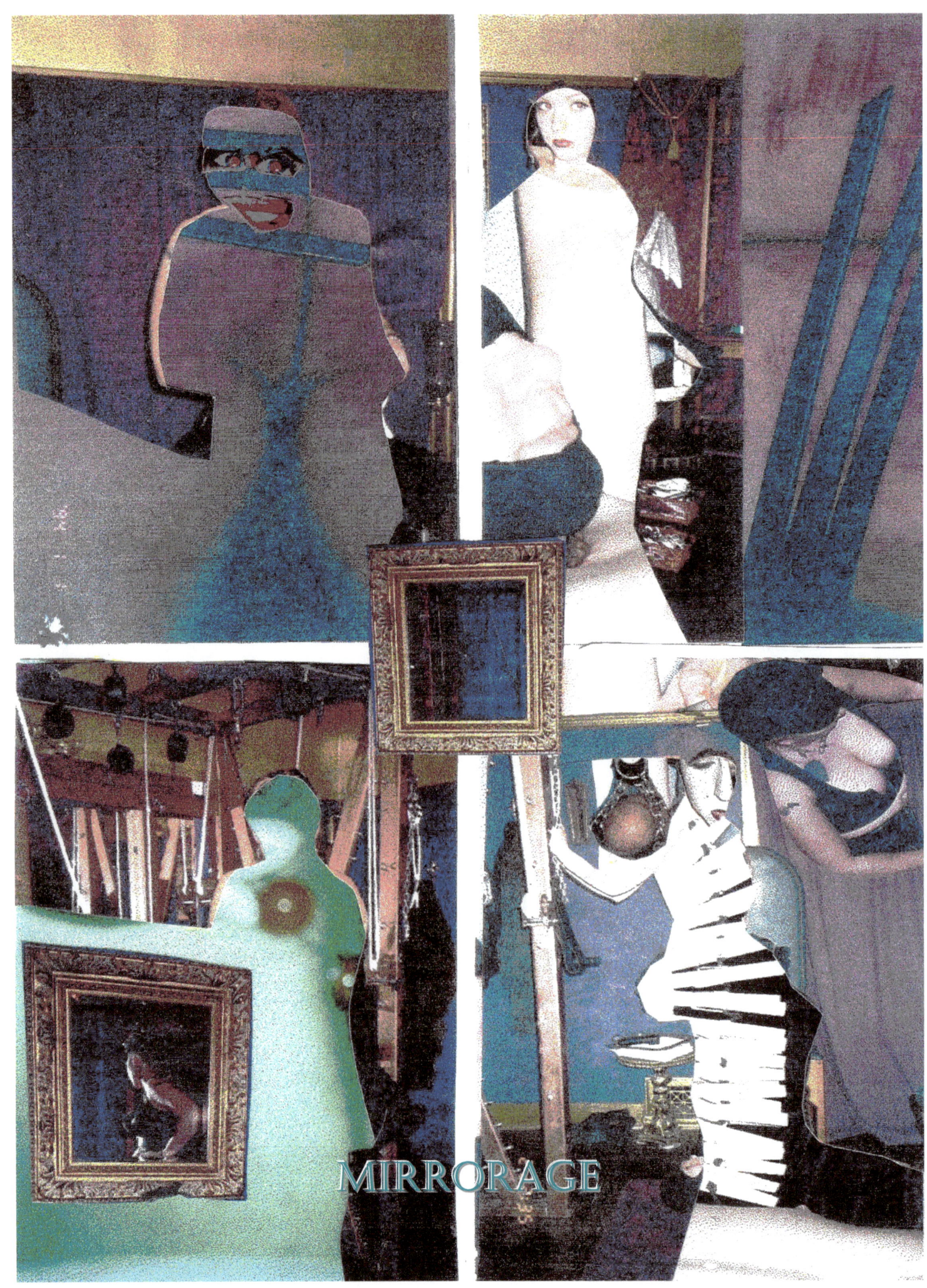

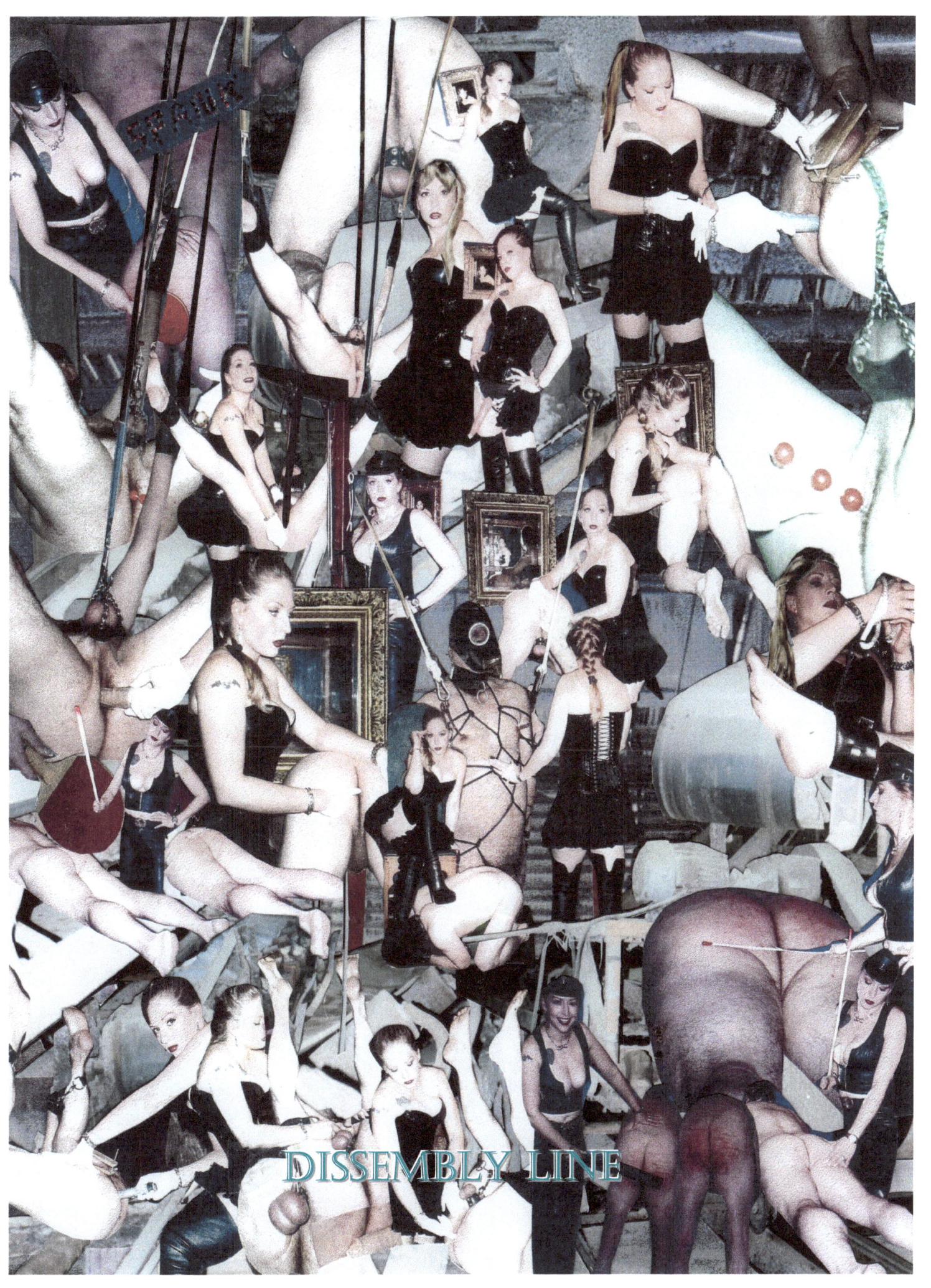

DISSEMBLY LINE

Chapter 10
DISMEMBRANCE
Triptych

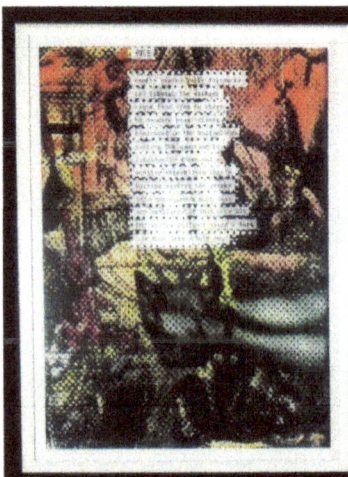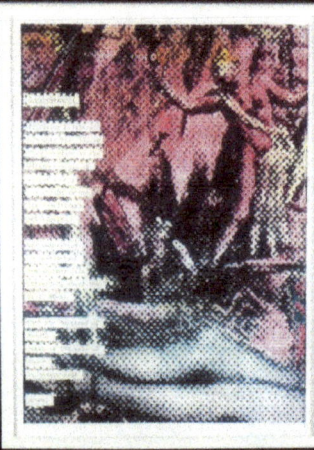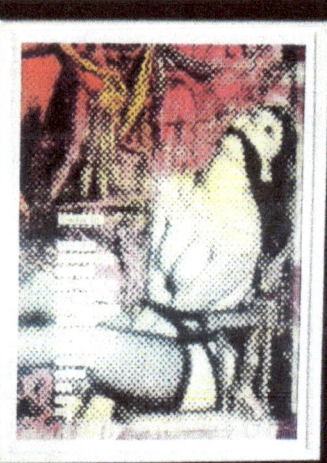

And they had as queen under them the Illustrix, Ms. von Kix, without whom their sky would not gleam fuzzy white silver hub cap diamond star halo.

The *genpop* were mostly *communicable*—"positive **mutaminants**"—and so were mostly *recycled* en masse. The *Immunicable*, though, they were **topside** rejects. They just didn't respond to the everecho's jittery barrage of debilitating neurolinguistics...whether victor or victim, they were marked for absconsion by the Catherine Society, who, like a rapture gone south down a spider hole, deposited at the feet of Madam's Mechanical Absolutions a balance of books by eking out to the last breath Displacement Credits for the **youb** who might otherwise infect all United Holy Humpdom if he were to query, say, his block's VeriCheX-ray Tech: *Would you like me to lift my sac? How 'bout my wife's floppy tits? Have my daughter **stick out** her butt'n'gina? How 'bout we **stick** a **feather duster** up your ass and call it* **Macaroni?**

The Breatharians foster all *nasty* because they **can.** Tourette's at the helm of the *Ecoplexus:* **Cock**efellers and Kiss**ass**ingers weigh each breath.

Newbie youbs begin their sentences warehoused in the drone stables. To feel the full frontal brunt of First Day at Kix Caverns is to feel the life force swell up out from the **magma** through toes up veins flowing forth **lava.**

The Ma'am said *glide* so we **glid.**

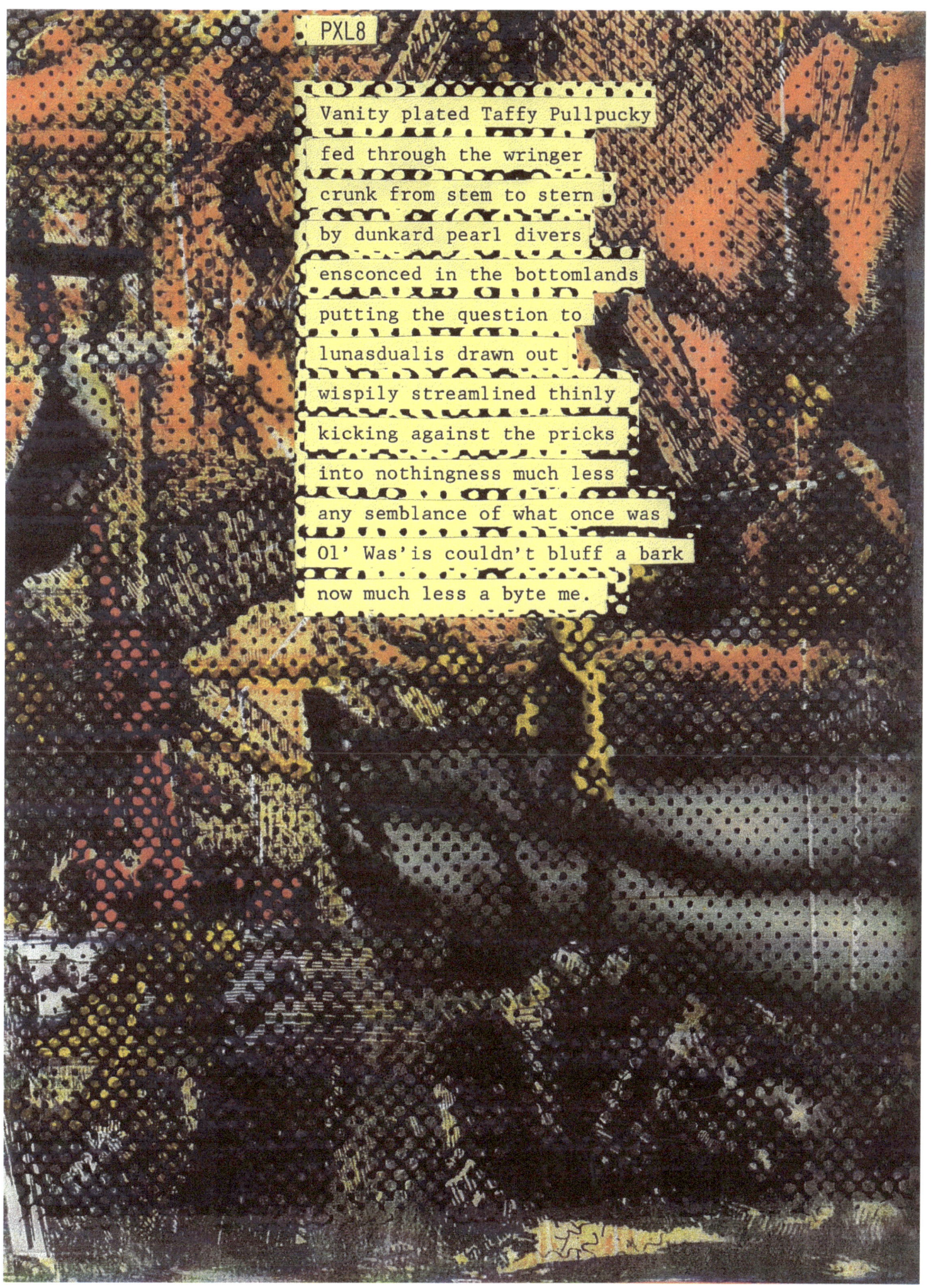

Vanity plated Taffy Pullpucky
fed through the wringer
crunk from stem to stern
by dunkard pearl divers
ensconced in the bottomlands
putting the question to
lunasdualis drawn out
wispily streamlined thinly
kicking against the pricks
into nothingness much less
any semblance of what once was
Ol' Was'is couldn't bluff a bark
now much less a byte me.

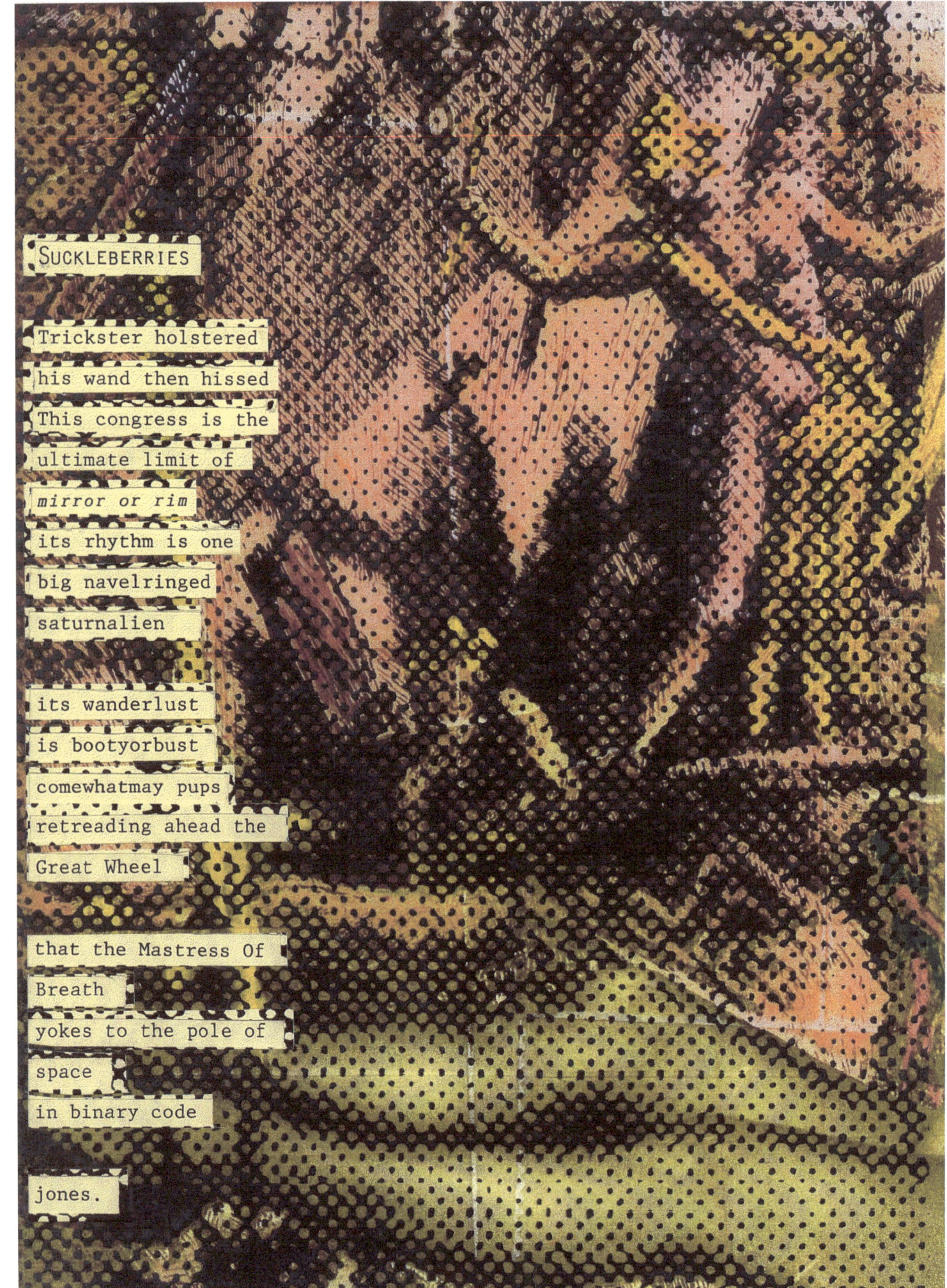

SUCKLEBERRIES

Trickster holstered
his wand then hissed
This congress is the
ultimate limit of
mirror or rim
its rhythm is one
big navelringed
saturnalien

its wanderlust
is bootyorbust
comewhatmay pups
retreading ahead the
Great Wheel

that the Mastress Of
Breath
yokes to the pole of
space
in binary code

jones.

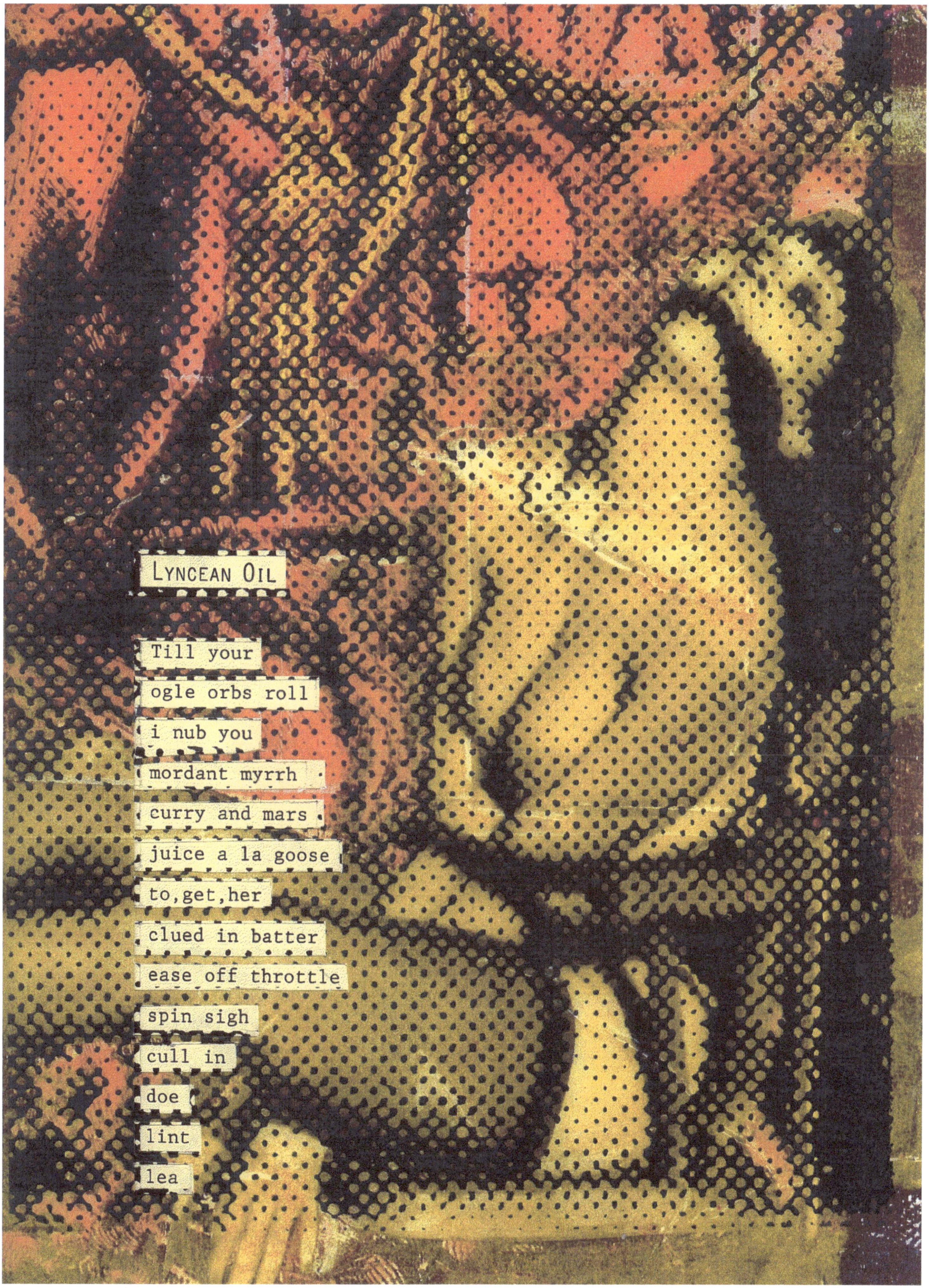

LYNCEAN OIL

Till your

ogle orbs roll

i nub you

mordant myrrh

curry and mars

juice a la goose

to,get,her

clued in batter

ease off throttle

spin sigh

cull in

doe

lint

lea

Finalé

Finally, a sequential art catalog that plays like metric montage spliced from a reconciled *opus interruptus* of pent up photo cut-ups while the *prima modella*, Ilsa Strix, turns the tables in the Factory Street temple before Iz and she closed shop when Ilsa hooked up with another sequential artist, ~~Larry~~ Lana Wachowski, who so, as well, paid art's ultimate price.

The thread of this *Operotica* wends throughout the machinations of the Webstress Illustra von Kix conducting a power exchange, yin for yang, with the e*lsen* Doctor Mortsac, who so over amps their prison planet's exoskeletal Nidus Plexus that it fazes amok acoustic shadows until the "mash sheen eerie" descends into a cascading tessellation of crumbling dungeons strung to the bend in time. Be he victor or victim, in the end their argument is all just a matter of semantics, I'm sure.

ONEIROS BOOKS Edition
Published **March 8, 2014**

www.ingramcontent.com/pod-product-compliance
Lightning Source LLC
Chambersburg PA
CBHW050731180526

45159CB00003B/1193